# 'Tis some poor fellow's skull

# 'Tis some poor fellow's skull

◆

## Post-Soviet Warfare in the Southern Caucasus

*Patrick Wilson Gore*

*with photographs by Ruslan Sarkisian, combat photographer of Azat Artsakh, Stepanakert, and cartography by Michael Bechthold*

iUniverse, Inc.
New York  Lincoln  Shanghai

# 'Tis some poor fellow's skull
## Post-Soviet Warfare in the Southern Caucasus

iUniverse books may be ordered through booksellers or by contacting:

iUniverse
2021 Pine Lake Road, Suite 100
Lincoln, NE 68512
www.iuniverse.com
1-800-Authors (1-800-288-4677)

Front cover:  The Karvachar battleground, looking west from Gandzasar. Author's photograph.

ISBN: 978-0-595-48679-3 (pbk)
ISBN: 978-0-595-60775-4 (ebk)

Printed in the United States of America

"'Tis some poor fellow's skull," said he,
"Who fell in the great victory."

*After Blenheim,*
Robert Southey (1774-1843)

# Contents

# ACKNOWLEDGMENTS

"No names, no pack drill," said the old sweats of the British Expeditionary Force.

Many workers in the shadows who have been most helpful in compiling this history would not wish to see their names in print lest pack drill or some worse fate be their lot. So the author must limit himself to a general thank you, however inadequate this may seem. They know who they are and how much they have helped.

Thanks are also due to the Ministries of Defense and of Foreign Affairs of Nagorno-Karabagh for facilitating the author's access to the Republic, and specifically to front-line areas.

Apart from this help, no direct or indirect participant in the Nagorno-Karabagh conflict has contributed toward the publication of this book.

# A NOTE ON LANGUAGE AND TERMINOLOGY

Dozens of languages and dialects are spoken by the fifty ethnic groups that inhabit the Caucasus.

There are two Armenian languages, Eastern and Western, which linguists divide into a total of sixty-two dialects. Eastern Armenian dialects are spoken in the republics of Armenia and Nagorno-Karabagh and in parts of the Middle East where Armenian refugees settled. Western Armenian is widely spoken in the Western *Diaspora*, and by the last survivors of the two million[1] Armenians who lived in Turkey a century ago.

The very name of Nagorno-Karabagh, with which this book is chiefly concerned, is a blend of three other languages: *nagorno* is Russian for mountainous, *kara* is Turkic for black, and *bagh* is Persian for garden.

Nagorno-Karabagh was an autonomous *oblast* within Azerbaijan—a construct of Stalin. The name is now used by the young Armenian republic whose capital is Stepanakert. It consists of most, but not all, of Stalin's *oblast,* with the addition of enough adjacent territory to provide the Nagorno-Karabagh Republic with land access to the Republic of Armenia and with a defensible frontier.

The simpler and vaguer term, Karabagh, is used in this book to reflect an often fluid reality. The term *Karabaghtsi* is applied to the people of the area, Armenians who also call their homeland *Artsakh*.

The Nagorno-Karabagh Republic is now almost 100 per cent Armenian, a return to the situation that prevailed in 1920.

When the *oblast* was ruled by Baku, the Armenian presence was considered unfortunate. So after the ethnic cleansing of Nagorno-Karabagh that the Azeris undertook in 1991, Azeris who had been living in the Armenian Soviet Socialist Republic and Meskhetian Turks from Central Asia, were settled in formerly Armenian towns and villages to reduce the *oblast*'s overwhelmingly Armenian complexion.

Accurate numbers are elusive. Baku's statistics for the Communist and immediate post-Communist periods are not helpful. To take one example, they do not distinguish between Indo-European Kurds on the one hand, and Azeris on the other, and so show no Kurds at all in Azerbaijan.[2]

This was demonstrably inconsistent with reality, however much the Azeris might wish to represent Azerbaijan as an exclusively Azeri state.

In fact, the *Karabaghtsi* and the Kurds were only part of the problem the Azeris had with their minorities. Language spoken is often the most meaningful key to ethnicity and in Azerbaijan, Lezgi (a Northeastern Caucasian language), and Talish (an Iranian language) are spoken by thousands of people.

Millions, of course, speak Azerbaijani, which is an Altaic Turkic language, closely related to Turkish. However, most Azeri speakers (between 16 and 23 million of them) actually live in Iran where they represent a significant presence in a population of 70 million.

Azerbaijani has been written with three different alphabets within living memory.

Russian remains the *lingua franca* of the Caucasus. In many places, including Nagorno-Karabagh, it is still widely spoken and, at the time of the Karabagh War, was the language of command and control of the forces of the Nagorno-Karabagh Republic.

Many towns and villages in Karabagh have several names and various spellings of each. The present capital, for example, was called Khankendi until 1923, when it became Stepanakert in honor of a martyred Soviet hero.

So no two maps tell the same story. In a history of the ebb and flow of battle, this poses problems. Names in current, local use are preferred here, with the exception of those which were so widely used during the Karabagh War that to use any other would be confusing or seem pedantic. Lachin is now called Berdzor, for example, but the Lachin Corridor was of such strategic importance during the fighting that the name Lachin has been retained.

# INTRODUCTION

The Mrav Mountains divide Azerbaijan's western panhandle from the Armenian lands to the south.

The Mrav's southern slopes are still littered with the bones of a shattered army of conscripts, largely drawn from Azerbaijan's minority communities, Kurds, Talish, and Lesgins, with a leavening of poor Azeri youths who couldn't afford to bribe their way off the draft list, or weren't fleet enough of foot to avoid the press gang.

The army had marched at the behest of Baku politicians who had sworn to bring to heel another of Azerbaijan's minorities, the Armenians of Nagorno-Karabagh, who after seventy years of Baku rule, had concluded that they would be more likely to survive in neighboring Armenia than in post-Soviet Azerbaijan.

That was a lesson drawn from their long experience as second-class citizens in the Azerbaijan Soviet Socialist Republic. They had no reason to believe that things would be better in the 1990s, now that the Baku politicians were free of Moscow's restraining hand; every reason to think that things would be much worse.

# ORIGINS OF THE KARABAGH WAR

When the Union of Soviet Socialist Republics disintegrated in the late 1980s, some outcomes were predictable, others less so. The Baltic republics had two decades of experience as Western-style democracies behind them—between the First and Second World Wars. No one was surprised when they left the Soviet Union relatively painlessly.

In other cases, the Communists bequeathed poison pills to their successor regimes, usually involving some gerrymandered frontier that did not match ethnic realities or reasonable national aspirations.

The sinister hand of Stalin, Commissar of Nationalities in the Moscow Council of People's Commissars from 1917 to 1924, can be seen clearly in some situations.[3] In others, Moscow made mistakes, such as that which cost Russia the home port of its Black Sea Fleet. Twice in a century, Russia shed buckets of blood to defend the Hero-City of Sevastopol, only to lose the great naval base through carelessness.[4]

At the beginning of the 21st century, the only ongoing "hot" war in what used to be the Soviet Union is the second round of hostilities, no longer confined to the North Caucasus Military District, between the Russian Federation and various Chechen factions. However, from the Dniester to Central Asia, there are points of friction that have been, or could easily become battlegrounds.

Small wars sometimes become big wars, but this post-Soviet instability matters particularly because, unless there is some unforseen breakthrough in energy technology, whoever has control over, or even access to, the vast oil and natural gas reserves under the Caspian and in Central Asia[5], will have a powerful influence on the history of the 21st century.

Moreover, between the High Arctic and the Tropic of Cancer, there is only one 100-mile-wide corridor connecting Europe and Asia, that is not controlled by either Russia or Iran. Karabagh lies in the middle of this choke-point through which all non-Russian oil and gas pipelines must be routed, and through which all American and Coalition military aircraft bound to or from Afghanistan, Pakistan or Central Asia must fly if they are to avoid Russian and Iranian air space.[6]

◆    ◆    ◆

At the south-western extremity of what the Russians call their "near abroad", Moldova lies between the Ukraine and Romania. Two-thirds of those who live in what used to be the Moldavian Soviet Socialist Republic consider themselves Moldavian or Romanian, but others are Russian by speech and culture, and do not have any intention of becoming anything else. Their republic of Transnistria, centered on Tiraspol, is recognized by no one but the citizens of other orphan states, but, thanks to the material legacy of the Soviet 14th Army, lingering on as the Operational Group of Russian Forces in Moldova, it is the most heavily armed region of its size anywhere in the world.

Building on this legacy, according to the Brussels-based International Crisis Group, Transnistria now has five or six factories making small arms, mortars and missile-launchers for export.

On the opposite shore of the Black Sea, Georgia seems to have resolved its problem with Adjara, but has two other secessionist states to deal with, Abkhazia and South Ossetia. And the Chechen War regularly spills over into the Pankisi Gorge in north-eastern Georgia, where the population is Kist—ethnically Chechen.

The Gorge, refuge for transnational criminals, Wahhabi terrorists[7], and Chechen guerrillas, is a volatile place. If Russia needs an excuse to move back into the Southern Caucasus, it will likely find it here.

The problems between the Armenians and the Azeris in Karabagh result from the fact that the two peoples, plus an admixture of Kurds, have for centuries been scattered higgledy-piggledy across the Southern Caucasus landscape, in some cases even sharing villages.

Further east, similar confusion exists in the Ferghana Valley, shared among Uzbekistan, Kyrgyzstan and Tadžikistan. Post-Soviet elites are aligned by clan, by bonds of corruption, by inertia; aligned by anything but a desire to seek stability and avert the possibility that Central Asia will turn into a powerhouse of militant Islamic fundamentalism.

Two thousand died in 1992 when Uzbeks and Kyrgyz clashed in Osh in Kyrgyzstan, and estimates of the dead in the civil war between northern and southern Tadžik clans run as high as 100,000.

Many potentially explosive situations have been defused as a result of the voluntary or involuntary exile from their old homes of people who do not match the complexion of the government of the day. In some cases, these refugees, or internally displaced persons, have settled into new homes; in others, their plight is wretched.

◆     ◆     ◆

The promise of *perestroika* and the subsequent collapse of the Soviet Empire provided citizens of its component republics an opportunity to think about what an ideal post-Soviet world might look like.

One thing the Armenians who lived in the mountains of western Azerbaijan knew for sure was that they could not remain Azeri citizens and survive.

Although Armenia and Azerbaijan were then sovereign (though Communist) states[8], Stalin gave Nagorno-Karabagh to Azerbaijan in 1921 as a gesture of conciliation to Kemal Ataturk, who (Moscow hoped) might yet prove to be more socialist than nationalist Turk. This despite the fact that the Revolutionary Committee of Azerbaijan had already recognized that Nagorno-Karabagh was a part of neighboring Armenia for the good and sufficient reason that Karabagh was 94 per cent Armenian at that time.[9]

So Nagorno-Karabagh became an autonomous *oblast* within the Azerbaijan Soviet Socialist Republic, but the region did not prosper under Baku's rule. All important decisions were made in Baku by Azeris who saw Nagorno-Karabagh as no more than a source of raw materials to be exploited for the benefit of the Baku *nomenklatura*. A hold was put on any real economic development, such as copper and gold mining at Drmbon, that might have benefitted the Armenians who lived there.

But Armenians and Azeris had all been Soviet citizens; Moscow had always been there to see some kind of justice done. Until now.

Now, second-class citizenship in Azerbaijan, without Moscow mediation, was a terrifying prospect. For in Armenian eyes, the Azeris were Turks; they spoke a language indistinguishable from Turkish and readily adopted what the Armenians perceived to be Turkish practices, like ethnic cleansing and genocide. The Armenians had not forgotten the stories of how, at the end of the 19th century and beginning of the 20th, the Turks had massacred between one and two million Armenians. As many as 30,000 died in Baku alone in September 1918, according to the German intelligence officer, Wilhelm Litten.[10]

The Turks, with the notable exceptions of Nobel laureate Orhan Pamuk[11] and Professor Taner Akçam[12], deny there was any genocide. They claim that the Armenians constituted a dangerous "fifth column" (to use a phrase that gained currency during the Spanish Civil War) behind their lines as they battled the Tsar's armies at Sarikamish, and that any measures they took against the Armenians were necessary and reasonable in time of war.

As for Baku, the Armenians and Bolsheviks had cleared the city of Azeris in April 1918, with great bloodshed. The Turks say that the grisly events of September 1918 were predictable payback.

But even today, many Armenians think of the Azeris as Turks with the same skin-crawling dread and revulsion that a survivor of Auschwitz might have for a Sieg-heiling Nazi.

In fact, Azeri Communist Party boss Heidar Aliev[13] boasted of being "the first Turk in the Politburo" in 1982 when Andropov made him a First Deputy Prime Minister of the USSR. And Azeris and Anatolian Turks do speak mutually-intelligible Turkic languages, and are related ethnically. Since 1992 both Turks and Azeris have used the same Western alphabet.

The gathering of all Turkic speakers into an empire to be called Turan is a key element in the platform of the Turkey's Nationalist Action Party. The party's militants, the Gray Wolves, were very visible in the Azerbaijan government and military at various times during the Karabagh War.

Pro-Turkish and pro-Russian regimes came and went in Baku in the 1990s, but neither secular Turks nor post-Soviet Azeris seemed inclined to let the fact that the Turks are traditionally Sunni Moslems and the Azeris Shiite, stand in the way of geostrategic cooperation. The Azeri army was, for example, supported during the Karabagh War by "advisors" from the regular Turkish army, including at least one general. These NATO-trained officers orchestrated the Azeri victories of the summer of 1992 that came close to wiping the Nagorno-Karabagh Republic off the map.

Despite the West's thirst for oil and natural gas, and heavy investment in pipeline construction, the great powers have been unable to come to grips with issues that emerged in the Southern Caucasus after the Soviet Union collapsed.

Yeltsin's Russia, of course, had problems closer to home, specifically in Chechnya, but the Clinton-Albright regime in the United States gave no sign of having any strategy in place to deal with post-Soviet issues, other than to cash in a "peace dividend".[14] In fact, the Central Intelligence Agency stopped monitoring newspapers in the region, one of the most economical and least intrusive ways of gathering intelligence, at a time when Tehran was rumored to be moving 1,300 agents into Azerbaijan.[15]

However, the Israeli *Mossad,* which intermittently shares intelligence with the Central Intelligence Agency, has systematically nurtured anti-Tehran sentiments among the millions of Azeris who live in northwest Iran, acquiring useful information from both sides of the Azerbaijan-Iran frontier in the process.

As long as American and Israeli interests remained closely aligned, Washington was able to live with this dependence on a foreign intelligence service.

# ECONOMIC BACKGROUND

The Karabagh War between Armenian and Azeri was played out against a background of economic concerns, and from the beginning economic weapons were used when opportunity arose.

In 1989 the Azeris imposed a blockade on traffic from Azerbaijan to Armenia, with the intent of forcing Yerevan to stop encouraging the secessionist aspirations of Nagorno-Karabagh. Rail service to Stepanakert was also terminated.

As most of Armenia's international trade, including 85 per cent of oil imports, passed through Baku, the blockade represented a body blow to the country's economy, which was already reeling as a result of the Spitak earthquake of December 1988.

The Spitak earthquake measured 6.8 on the Richter scale and left at least 25,000 dead[16] and many communities devastated, including Gyumri, Armenia's second largest city. Sixty per cent of the buildings there were destroyed or made uninhabitable. Half-a-million Armenians were left homeless, and the Metsamor nuclear plant had to be taken off-line in March 1989.

Metsamor, built in 1977, had two VVER-440/230 light-water reactors. They were probably safer than Chernobyl's graphite-moderated and water-cooled installation, but the Armenian plant was considered vulnerable to further shocks.

As Metsamor produced most of Armenia's electricity, the country had little power for several years. Only in October 1995 was it possible to restart one of the reactors.

During the first winters of the blockade, both Armenian populations suffered considerable privation. So serious was the shortage of electricity and other fuel in Yerevan, that stories are told of people drawing power from the city's priority 600-volt streetcar supply to boil water for their morning tea. They would attach a razor-blade to a wire that was tossed across the positive live cable that powered the trams. The razor blade was suspended in a metal pot of water sitting on the negative ground rail. The thin blade would heat up quickly and boil the water.[17]

Although Karabagh suffered more severely than Armenia as a result of bombardment and invasion, it did fare better in terms of electricity supply after 1993. At the end of February 1993, Karabagh forces captured the Sarsang Reservoir and hydro-electric plant, and over the next year restored electric power to the whole Nagorno-Karabagh Republic. The lack of any transmission infrastructure, however, made it impossible in the short term to provide power to Armenia.

The blockade continues to impose serious constraints on the economic development of both Armenia and Nagorno-Karabagh, and provides the Azeris with considerable leverage in negotiations.

The Azeris have leverage, but not enough to re-establish Azeri control over Nagorno-Karabagh. As soon as Armenian President Levon Ter-Petrosian was seen to be buckling under Azeri pressure in 1998, he was replaced in Yerevan by the hard-line *Karabaghtsi*, Robert Kocharian[18], who had briefly served under him as prime minister of Armenia.

Data are elusive, but since the blockade was imposed, considerable numbers of Armenians have left their homelands to find work in the West, following in the footsteps of those who fled Anatolia during the *Diaspora* of the early 20th century. Their remittances, like those of the earlier *Diaspora*, together with a certain grim courage, enable the two Armenian states to survive.

Armenia and Nagorno-Karabagh both worked hard to resettle approximately 260,000 refugees who fled westward from Azerbaijan after the latest *pogroms* began in 1988. The total number of Armenians who escaped is hard to quantify as the Armenians of Azerbaijan often spoke better Russian than Armenian, and many fled to Russia to escape the *pogroms*, rather than to blockaded Armenia or Nagorno-Karabagh.[19]

Azerbaijan, on the other hand, has taken the position that any resettlement of Azeris who used to live in Armenia or in territory now controlled by the Nagorno-Karabagh Republic, would represent an admission that land beyond the 1994 cease-fire line had been lost for good. Consequently an estimated 700,000[20] Azeri refugees still live in camps, railroad yards, or elsewhere, in temporary dwellings, often in conditions of considerable hardship that seem incomprehensible in oil-rich Azerbaijan.[21]

Tengiz Kodrarian, a journalist who has traveled widely in Azerbaijan, writes of "several hundreds of thousands of refugees....kept in cemeteries created for the living, refugees in their own land"[22].

Azeri politicians complain that the Nagorno-Karabagh forces occupy upwards of one fifth of what had been Azerbaijan during the Soviet era, but Tom de Waal calculates the lost area at under 14 per cent, including Nagorno-Karabagh itself.[23]

# THE BATTLEFIELD

The Lesser Caucasus mountains drop quite abruptly to the valley of the River Kura. Although Moslem Tartars or Azeris, and Christian Armenians have lived together throughout Karabagh, sharing territory and sometimes living as neighbors, it is generally true to say that the Armenians live in the mountains of Nagorno-Karabagh, while the Azeris occupy the broad river valleys below.

The situation is, however, complicated by the fact that before the Communist Revolution, many Tartars, as the Azeris were generally called in those days, were to some extent nomadic and practiced transhumance, moving their herds up to the green mountains of Karabagh in the summer and down to the plains in winter.

During the Soviet era, the *oblast*, or autonomous region, of Nagorno-Karabagh was an area shaped somewhat like a figure eight, stretching a maximum of 120 miles from north to south, and 50 miles, more or less, from east to west. It had an area of about 1,700 square miles.

To the west, the Republic of Armenia is more than twice as big as the *oblast*, being slightly smaller than the state of Maryland.

The southwest border of the Nagorno-Karabagh *oblast* came to within a few miles of the Republic of Armenia, with only the town of Lachin to separate the two Armenian regions. Lachin was a key communications center, sitting on the main road from the Armenian frontier up the Lachin Corridor to Stepanakert. A secondary road led from Lachin into southern Azerbaijan and to the border with Iran. Other roads ran east and southeast from Stepanakert to Martuni and to Ghadrut respectively.

Lachin has changed hands a number of times. The archeologist Samvel Karapetian claims, on the basis of his study of ancient inscriptions and other discoveries, that it was an Armenian town for centuries.[24] Kurds and Azeris have also lived there, and in the neighboring villages.

The backbone of Nagorno-Karabagh was the road that led from Goris in the Republic of Armenia through Lachin to Stepanakert, the modern capital of Nagorno-Karabagh, and on to Mardakert or, forking east, to Aghdam. From Aghdam, another road looped down along the eastern border of the *oblast* to Dzhebrail, with the Karabagh mountains to the west and the Azeri lowlands to the east.

The southeast frontier of the Nagorno-Karabagh *oblast* was about 20 miles, at its closest, from the River Araks, the major tributary of the Kura which separated Azerbaijan from Iran at this point.

Three other rivers rise in the Karvachar mountains between the Nagorno-Karabagh *oblast* and Armenia's eastern frontier. The Tartar and the Khachenaget flow eastward to add their waters eventually to those of the River Kura.

In the north, the Tartar had been dammed during the Soviet era to form the Sarsang Reservoir and generate hydro-electric power. A road ran up the Tartar valley into the sparsely-inhabited mountains of Karvachar, which had not been assigned to Nagorno-Karabagh, and which, in the 1920s, Stalin considered turning into a "Red Kurdistan".

A road also ran up the valley of the Khachenaget River as far as the Karvachar border.

The southern part of Karvachar drains southward into the third river, the Akera, which eventually flows into the Araks.

The watershed between the river basins of northern and southern Karvachar rises at Dalidagh to almost 12,000 feet. No roads cross it.

*Nagorno* means mountainous in Russian; the region is well named. The mountains are broken by valleys and basins like that in which Stepanakert lies, but the only real lowland is in the east.

The Mrav Mountains, the north-eastern range of the Lesser Caucasus, rise to 12,200 feet above sea level. The unpredictable and occasionally brutal weather in these mountains was a key factor in the last phase of military operations there.

By May 1994, the Nagorno-Karabagh government controlled about 4,500 square miles, inhabited by an estimated 160,000 people. Ninety-five per cent were Armenian, with the balance made up of Russians, Kurds and Azeris.

But in May 2000, Anushavan Danielian, prime minister of the Nagorno-Karabagh Republic, told Tom de Waal that the population of the republic was a state secret.[25]

# THE COMBATANTS

The Caucasus, where Europe and Asia meet, is home to fifty nations and hundreds of clans. Persian, Ottoman and Russian Empires collided here; frontiers remained fluid until the Cold War set them in concrete.

The most numerous peoples of the Southern Caucasus are the Georgians, the Armenians and the Azeris.

But only half of the world's Armenians live in Armenia and Karabagh, together with some Yezidi Kurds[26] and a handful of Russians. The other half, the *Diaspora* Armenians, live all over the world; Armenian can be heard in the streets of Buenos Aires, Sydney, Fresno, and Paris, as well as in Tehran, Beirut and Moscow.

Neither the Georgians nor the Azeris have wandered so far afield in such numbers, although one Georgian, Joseph Vissarionovich Dzhugashvili (1879-1953), better known as Stalin, dominated the USSR for a quarter of a century.

During the early years of Communist rule, Stalin, responsible for the Nationalities portfolio, understood that Moscow's power depended on fragmenting any possible nucleii of resistance. The Armenians, for example, would be less likely to cause trouble if they were split between two subordinate Soviet Socialist Republics, Armenia and Azerbaijan.

Furthermore, any gesture that appeared to favor the Turkic-speaking Azeris, might be seen favorably by Kemal Ataturk, whose goodwill was important to the Bolsheviks at a time when their hold on the Southern Caucasus was still tenuous. British agents and even a British expeditionary force[27] had been operating on the southern Caspian littoral, tempted there by Baku oil.

In his famous painting of the execution of Stepan Shaumian[28] and the other Baku commissars, Isaac Brodsky shows uniformed British officers supervising the firing squad. In fact, the British were not involved in killing the twenty-six commissars, but the painting reflects Soviet nervousness about foreign threats to the Caspian oilfields.

So it was that Stalin assigned the Armenians of Karabagh to Azerbaijan, although the Armenian heartland was only a few miles south and west of what became the Azerbaijan SSR *oblast* of Nagorno-Karabagh. From those early years, Azeri policy sought to distance Nagorno-Karabagh from Armenia, even to the extent of allowing the only motor road between Armenia and Nagorno-Karabagh to decay into impassability.

The disintegration of the Soviet Union in 1991 obliged non-Russians who had made careers in the USSR to decide whether to remain in Moscow or wherever else they had located, or to return to their homelands. As neither Russia nor post-earthquake Armenia was in good shape economically, the choice might not have been easy for Armenians, but Azeris could hope that the Caspian oil and natural gas reserves would fuel a bright future for Azerbaijan and particularly for the once-great, cosmopolitan city of Baku.

◆    ◆    ◆

Even in Khrushchev's day, reports of Karabagh grievances reached Moscow, where they were routinely ignored. Then in the *glasnost* and *perestroika* years of the 1980s, there were ever louder calls for reunification of the two Armenian communities.

At the outset, few Armenians wanted independence from Russia. Turkey was altogether too close, and the international community's inability to dislodge the Turkish army from Northern Cyprus after the 1974 invasion, provided a lesson not lost on the Armenians.

Of course, the Azeris continued to argue against any consideration of Karabagh demands, playing the card of "territorial integrity", which in international fora would usually trump ephemeral concepts like self-determination, and freedom from fear of imminent genocide. The deal on Nagorno-Karabagh was done, and the decision taken, even if it had been taken by Stalin, and for questionable reasons.

History condemns almost everything else that Stalin did, from extermination of the *kulaks* to development of the *Gulag* system, but, through the lens of political expediency, the international community determines that he was right where Nagorno-Karabagh was concerned.

Specialists in international law take a different approach. According to an analysis by New England School of Law's Center for International Law and Policy, and the Public International Law and Policy Group:

"Nagorno Karabagh has a right of self-determination, including the attendant right to independence, according to the criteria recognized under international law.... The principle of self-determination is included in the United Nations Charter, [and] was further codified in the International Covenant on Civil and Political Rights, and the International Covenant on Economic, Social and Cultural Rights ... The right to self-determination has also been repeatedly recognized in a series of resolutions adopted by the U.N. General Assembly."

The analysis further notes that, as the Nagorno-Karabagh Republic's "independence was declared not from the Soviet Union but from Azerbaijan," and as Nagorno-Karabakh "at that time was part of a still existent and internationally recognized Soviet Union," the Nagorno-Karabagh Republic's declaration of independence "fully complied with existing law".

This was because "the 1990 Soviet law titled *Law of the USSR Concerning the Procedure of Secession of a Soviet Republic from the USSR* provides that the secession of a Soviet republic (such as Azerbaijan) from the body of the USSR allows an autonomous region and compactly settled minority regions in the same republic's territory also to trigger their own process of independence."

Furthermore, "the USSR Constitutional Oversight Committee did not annul the declaration establishing the Nagorno-Karabagh Republic, since that declaration was deemed in compliance with the then existing law."

◆     ◆     ◆

But to view the Nagorno-Karabagh War as a conflict between Karabagh and Azeri forces involves an oversimplification.

Two combatants are enough to fight a war, but the war in the Southern Caucasus was particularly complicated. Always behind Karabagh stood the Armenians of the Yerevan republic and of the *Diaspora*.

At a further remove, the Turks stood behind the Azeris, certainly in the perception of the average Armenian. With its echoes of 1915, *Operation Koltso*, the ethnic-cleansing operation initiated by the special forces of the Azeri Interior Ministry in the spring of 1991, removed any doubts the Karabagh people might have had about how much trouble they were in.

The other side of the Armenian genocide coin was resistance to the Turks. The Armenians had a tradition of resistance for, long before the First World War, Armenians had organized themselves, and many took up arms.

Andranik Toros Ozanian is the best known of those early freedom fighters. In 1887, at the age of twenty-two, he joined a resistance group in Shabin-Karahisar, his home in Turkey. When the group's commander was killed,

Andranik became its leader. By 1901 he was already a hero to the Armenians and anathema to the Turks.

Between 1907 and 1913 he fought in Bulgaria, where his Armenian volunteer battalion distinguished itself during the Balkan Wars against the Turks.

In 1914, the First World War pitted Russia against Turkey. Andranik, under Russian auspices, organized Armenian forces to fight the Turks closer to home. In 1915 he was named commander of all Armenian volunteers in the Russian army.

He ended the war as a major-general, but he was no more able than anyone else to bring order out of the ethnic and political chaos that overwhelmed the Caucasus as the Romanov and Ottoman empires collapsed, and as Ataturk and Lenin emerged. He went to California like many of his compatriots of the *Diaspora* and died there in 1927, mourned as a national hero.

His exploits inspired a new generation of Armenians in the 1990s who found themselves fighting Azeris, proxy Turks. There were even a few in Nagorno-Karabagh, like the *Dashnak*, Pavlik Manochian, who wore the Caucasian short sword, the *kinjal*, and adopted the colorful dress and mustaches of Andranik's men, when all around him wore the drab, late-Soviet, *afghanka* gear.

In the months that followed the July 1988 vote by the Nagorno-Karabagh soviet to secede from Azerbaijan, the *Karabaghtsi*, together with an increasing flow of Armenian refugees from more vulnerable parts of Azerbaijan, started to form self-defense units.

They called themselves *fedayner*, a term of Arabic origin that had been adopted by Armenians ready to sacrifice their lives to resist genocidal Turks in 1915.[29] From the beginning, there was some coordination of operations among the companies of *fedayner*[30] although most Armenians in Nagorno-Karabagh and in the Republic of Armenia, just over the mountains, hoped that conflict could be averted. They were in no shape to fight a war, or even to defend themselves.

Despite serious problems in post-earthquake Armenia, Yerevan was the most immediate source of help for the *Karabaghtsi*. The Armenian Army of Independence (AAI) was founded there in 1989 by Leonid Azgaldian, killed in action in Karabagh in 1993, and by Levon Eiramjiants. It became a political party, and its members were mustered into the Interior Ministry forces when Armenia became independent from the Soviet Union on 21 September 1991.

Another Yerevan formation, the Armenian National Army (ANA), founded there in the same year as the AAI, by Razmik Vasilian and Vartan Vartanian, was purged by President Levon Ter-Petrosian in 1990.

Help for the *Karabaghtsi* also came from the *Diaspora*. There were no International Brigades, like those of the Spanish Civil War, but Armenians from the Middle East, from France and from the United States did play significant roles. One of those was Vicken Zakarian (1969-92), from the Armenian Youth Federation of Lebanon. He was killed at Lisagor in the Shoushi campaign.

The Armenian Youth Federation was a branch of the *Dashnaktsutiun,* the Armenian Revolutionary Federation (ARF), which was founded in Tblisi in 1890 by Kristofor Mikaelian, Stepan Zorian, and Simon Zavarian, to resist Turkish oppression and proclaim the ideals of social justice and democracy.

They were guerrilla fighters in the last days of the Ottoman Empire and established the short-lived Armenian Republic of 1918. When it collapsed under Bolshevik pressure in December 1920, the anti-Communist *Dash-naks* became a party of the *Diaspora*, only returning to the Caucasus after the collapse of the Soviet Empire. They played an important military and financial role in the Karabagh War, then found themselves banned in Armenia during the Ter-Petrosian regime from 1994 to 1998.

The Armenian Secret Army for the Liberation of Armenia (ASALA) formed in 1975 and headquartered first in Beirut then, after 1982, in Syria, represented another aspect of the Armenian *Diaspora*. ASALA was Marxist-Leninist and one of its leaders, the Armenian-American Monte Melkonian, became one of the heroes of the Karabagh War.

Most of the Armenians who left the Caucasus during the Soviet era had moved to other parts of the Soviet Union. Many had risen to positions of considerable importance in the USSR in government, the military, science and technology, and in the arts.

They did not return to Armenia in great numbers when the USSR broke up, but as the crisis deepened in Nagorno-Karabagh, a number of soldiers of Armenian origin rallied to the cause, including Kristofor Ivanian and Norat Ter-Grigoriants, a former Soviet deputy chief of staff, who became commander of the Armenian army.

Always in the background, stood the ex-Soviet army as well as the similarly uniformed and armed troops of the MVD, the *Ministerstvo Vnutrennikh Del* (Ministry of Internal Affairs). Estimates of MVD strength during the early 1990s vary around half-a-million but, as was the case with the army, much of the serious MVD work (in Chechnya, for example) was done by *kontraktniki*.[31] These were often former members of the MVD, who might or might not be listed in official totals. Both army and MVD were ethnically heterogeneous, although the Russian and European elements of Soviet society traditionally dominated the senior ranks.

One MVD officer who rallied to the Karabagh cause was Vagho Beglarian. He fought with great distinction on the Mardakert front and in the east.

Although the 31$^{st}$ Guards Motor Rifle Division headquartered in Gandža, was heavily Azeri, the same was not true of one of its component regiments. In fact, the commander of the 2$^{nd}$ Battalion of the 366$^{th}$ Motor Rifle Regiment in Stepanakert, Maj. Seiran Ohanian, after playing an important part in the Karabagh war, and his eventual promotion to major-general, became minister of defense of the Republic of Nagorno-Karabagh.

Ohanian was one of over a hundred Armenian officers and men of the 366$^{th}$ who transferred their allegiance, and some of the division's T-72 tanks, to the young Nagorno-Karabagh Republic when the Soviet Union fell apart. The remainder of the 366$^{th}$ was withdrawn to Georgia to be disbanded.[32]

And not all those who stayed behind were Armenians. One lieutenant-colonel, known to us as Yuri Nikolayevich,[33] had been deputy-commander of the 366$^{th}$. He assured his welcome in Nagorno-Karabagh by bringing over a considerable amount of useful hardware. He is remembered in Stepanakert as a skilled small arms instructor. Other ex-Soviet officers who helped the Armenian cause in Karabagh included the Russian Anatoly Zenevich, as well as a number of more junior Russians and Ukrainians who fought as adventurers or *kontraktniki*.

One Blue Beret[34] captain, known only as Valery, had a different take on the situation, particularly interesting in the light of subsequent events. He was from Mogilev in Belarus, but had served as a Soviet "advisor" in Somalia.

Most combatants on both sides rejected the view that the Karabagh War had a religious component. Not Valery. He believed in an Islamic threat, and that Islam had to be stopped in Karabagh. "If not," he told Paul Quinn-Judge of *The Boston Globe*, "I'll have to fight them in Belarus."[35]

Valery commanded a battalion of border guards, made up initially of ex-Soviet Armenian troops.

❖     ❖     ❖

In a sense, Stalin was right in seeing a difference between the *Karabaghtsi* and Yerevan Armenians. Both speak the Eastern Armenian tongue but the *Karabaghtsi* have a distinctive accent, with the stress falling toward the end of each word. Having been isolated from other Armenians for several generations, they use many more loan words from Russian and Azeri. Turkish and Persian have also influenced their speech.

The Yerevan Armenian will often call the *Karabaghtsi* 'ishaq' or mule, because of his proverbial stubbornness or determination, a characteristic that may explain to some extent why Karabagh produced a disproportionate number of marshals or admirals of the Soviet Union in the 20[36], and sent one of the first Armenians into space. Dr. James P. Bagian, who joined the U.S. National Aeronautics and Space Administration in 1978, is of Karabagh origin.

❖     ❖     ❖

Azerbaijan is the homeland of the Tartars[37], but Kurds, Talish and Lezgins also live within its borders. More Azeris actually live in Iran than in Azerbaijan, and the Azeri population in Georgia will number half-a-million in the foreseeable future.

So, as the Soviet Empire collapsed, Azerbaijan's ethnic diversity and the centrifugal tendencies of some significant minorities added another dimension of complexity to the problems faced by the central government in Baku.

One of these minorities merits particular notice, although Azeri census data do not distinguish between Kurds and any other native of Azerbaijan. During the 1990s, most Kurdish aspirations found their expression in building the de facto Kurdish state in northern Iraq, or in the ongoing low-intensity war in eastern Turkey.

Unlike some of the other minorities in Azerbaijan, the Kurds did not cause many problems for Baku, although Azeri army officers complained that Kurdish conscripts were poorly motivated. The same was certainly true of many Azeri conscripts, for Baku's system of conscription did not work well, at least not for the poor and marginalized. A bribe could assure indefinite exemption from the draft, and within the army there were reports of a culture of serious bullying of recruits analogous to the Soviet *dyedovshchina* system[38], and neglect by officers, tempered by corruption. Diseases such as tuberculosis, diphtheria and typhoid were reputed to be endemic in ill-maintained and dirty barracks, when barracks existed at all.

Other minorities well-represented in conscript ranks were the Talish and the Lesgins.

The Talish, an Iranian-speaking Shiite people, live beside the Caspian in southeastern Azerbaijan. Lenkoran is their capital.

The Husseinov coup in June 1993 and the chaos that ensued in Baku, gave Col. Aliakram Alekper Humbatov, a leader of Talish separatists who had formed his own brigade to fight the *Karabaghtsi*, a chance to proclaim a Talish-Mugam Republic, with himself as president.

But by August, Heidar Aliev was firmly in control in Baku and Humbatov had fled to Iran, extradition pending. The Talish had been brought under Azeri control again.

About 200,000 Lezgins live in northeastern Azerbaijan and an equal number across the Great Caucasus in southern Russia, where they constitute one of Daghestan's thirty ethnically and linguistically distinct peoples.

In Azerbaijan, they are Lezgins first and Azeris second. They are Moslem to be sure, but Sunni Moslem, at odds with the Shiite Azeris. Azerbaijan remains essentially a secular state, but the Shiite-Sunni split allows Baku to claim that the Lesgins have been led astray by the Wahhabis—Saudi fundamentalists blamed by the Russians for many of the problems they face in Chechnya, Daghestan's western neighbor.

Noting parallels between the situations of the Lesgins and of the *Karabaghtsi*, the Azeri security service claims to have evidence that Armenian agents have established links with the Lezgin secessionist organization *Sadval* (unity). Lesgin terrorists have been blamed for an attack on the Baku subway in March 1994, when four people died.

Oil revenues gave Azerbaijan the option of hiring professionals to operate the country's more sophisticated military equipment. Pilots, for example, were recruited from Russia, the Ukraine and Pakistan, to fly Azeri aircraft, as relatively few Azeris had the necessary training. For a variety of reasons, advancement in the more technical branches of the Soviet armed forces tended to be easier for Slavs than for Azeris and Central Asians, and the United States has provided training for the Pakistani armed forces.

The Baku regime found that foreign contract employees tended to be more competent and reliable than Azeri and minority conscripts. Bloodthirsty rhetoric in Baku drew thunderous applause but public enthusiasm for irredentism and genocide did not translate into voluntary enlistment in the Azeri army.

The extent to which the Azeris used Afghan troops in the war in Karabagh is unclear, although there is evidence that as many as 2,500 so-called *mujahidin* served with the Azeris. It was the Afghans who are said to have scorned their enemy as *asphalt fedayeen*.....an obscure obscure insult characterizing the *Karabaghtsi* as hillbillies just down from the mountains to fight for villages and towns, where they may have encountered paved roads for the first time.

The *Karabaghtsi*, many of whom had served in Afghanistan where the epithet was commonly applied to the *mujahidin*, called the Afghan mercenaries *dukhi* or simply savages.

There was some dialogue between the Azeri and Chechen leadership, and Shamil Basayev[39] was among the defenders of Shoushi, reportedly commanding a Chechen battalion. But there is no convincing evidence that any significant number of Chechens served with the Azeri forces at any time. Numbers of Chechens subsequently passed through Baku to fight as "insurgents" in Iraq.

Armenians and Azeris both say that the Russians aided their enemies, and stories are told of local Russian commanders, at various levels, who hired out their troops and tanks to whichever side could pay them. Stories, possibly apocryphal, circulate of individual tanks going into action for one side on one day, and for their enemies the next. The going daily rate for a T-72 and three-man crew was between $100 and $200 in United States currency; ammunition extra.

In the last resort, what would prove decisive was the superior motivation of the Armenian *azatamartic* or freedom-fighter, versus the *kontraktnik* and unwilling Azeri *asker*, led by a political class more focused on wrangling in Baku than on winning the war in Nagorno-Karabagh.

Throughout the Karabagh War, and even up to the time of writing, the internal politics of Azerbaijan have created an environment in which victory is hardly conceivable.

A president who saw himself as a cousin of the Turks, alternated with presidents whose ex-Soviet backgrounds and Russian sympathies seemed dominant. Within this framework, warlords roamed, alliances shifting from day to day. There were few constants, but among these, was the impossibility of abandoning Nagorno-Karabagh which Stalin had deeded to Azerbaijan. Perhaps the only other constant in Azerbaijan was endemic corruption.

Some of Azerbaijan's political parties played important roles during the Karabagh War.

The *Müsavat* (equality) Party was founded in Baku in 1911 by the journalist Muhammad Amin Rasulzade. Its ideology remains Pan-Turkic or Turanian, and it draws much support from Turkey. Strangely, one of the many colorful charges against the Mingrelian Lavrenti Beria[40] at the end of his life, was that he had once been a member of the Azeri *Müsavat*. He did not deny it.

There was, however, no ambiguity about Beria's position on Nagorno-Karabagh. It is reliably reported that he shot dead Aghasi Khanjian, Secretary of the Armenian Communist Party in the early 1930s, for taking a pro-Armenian position on the issue.[41]

The Nationalist Action Party played an important role in Azeri politics, as well as in Turkey itself. Its members were the Gray Wolves, who named their organization after *Bozkurt*, the Gray Wolf that is the mythic beast of Turkic legend. With his howl, *Bozkurt* summoned the Turks to migrate from Central Asia to the Caucasus and Anatolia.

The Armenians accuse the Grey Wolves of Azerbaijan of ritual cannibalism; of torturing, killing and eating young prisoners, or parts thereof, at *Qurban Bairam*, the Festival of Sacrifice.[42] True or not, the charge does nothing to dispel the loathing that so many Armenians and Azeris feel for each other.

The chairman of the center-right Azerbaijan National Independence Party (AMI), Etibar Mamedov, claimed that in the spring of 1992 he was involved, with the help of Turkish special forces, in transferring the equivalent of $500,000 in Turkish funds to Azerbaijan for the purchase of war matériel. Mamedov had about 2,000 men under arms in his own private army by mid-1992, when Abulfaz Aliev Elchibey[43], leader of another pro-Turkish party, the Azerbaijan Popular Front (APF), won the presidency.

Balancing the pro-Turkish parties was a strong contingent of pro-Russian Azeris. Ex-Soviet army and security service officers were to be found in Azeri ranks as well as with their enemies. Heidar Aliev and his henchman Vafa Guluzade both earned their spurs in the security apparatus of the USSR, but to label either as pro-Russian would be misleading.

As a young *chekist*, Aliev had served under Beria himself, although he actually started his career in Viktor S. Abakumov's Smersh (*Smert Shpionam* or 'death to spies') the agency responsible for the extermination of wartime collaborators. In this category Stalin included the two million Soviet prisoners-of-war that Truman and Churchill forcibly repatriated, pursuant to the Yalta agreement and its 31 March 1945 codicil.[44]

Aliev ended his security career as a KGB major-general, becoming the Communists' strong man in Azerbaijan as first secretary of the Azeri Central Committee. Tagged as "one of the great Communist dinosaurs" in the Gorbachev era, he was forced to retire from the Politburo "for health reasons" in October 1987, and went home to Nakhichevan.

Abulfaz Elchibey called him back to Baku in 1992 as deputy chairman of Azerbaijan's supreme council to shore up his weak and ineffective government. By June of that year he was chairman of the council, and, nine days later, president of Azerbaijan.

The story is told of an interview in Baku in late 1993 between Yeltsin's minister of defense, Pavel Grachev[45], and the newly-elected President Heidar Aliev, whose return to power had been welcomed by Moscow. Grachev laid out his demands; Aliev turned his KGB general's cold gaze on the Russian and explained that what Moscow wanted was supremely unimportant in Baku. The meeting left Grachev surprised and humiliated. Relations between Moscow and Baku deteriorated from that point.

By February 1995, Grachev was claiming that Azeri mercenaries were fighting in Chechnya for President Dzhokhar Dudayev, and Aliev was blaming Moscow for at least two abortive coups against him in Baku.

Some ex-Soviet officers, like Tajedin Mekhtiev, who was defense minister for nine weeks at the end of 1991 during the administration of Ayaz Mutalibov[46], spoke of the difficulties they faced in an Azeri administration that was totally preoccupied with political concerns that had little to do with winning the war in Nagorno-Karabagh, and which routed all its military communications through a switchboard controlled by Russian military intelligence.

At the local level, the situation was often as chaotic as it was in Baku. In the key communications center of Aghdam, for example, six or seven independent military units were in theory contributing to the Azeri war effort, but with no coordination at all. Sometimes they worked at cross purposes, or even in competition.

One notorious local commander was Yaqub Mamed; another was Asif Makhamerov, who was given the *nom de guerre* of *Freud,* because he was supposed to be an intellectual. Some leaders had some degree of credibility as a result of service in the Soviet army, others were gangsters pure and simple who saw the war, and breakdown of civilian authority, as a money-making opportunity.

The war was fought between communities that had lived cheek by jowl for centuries and it took some bizarre twists: During the assault on Khandzadzor, an Armenian defender felt a hand on his arm as he was drawing a bead on an Azeri attacker.

"Don't shoot," said the Armenian's comrade. "It's Ahmed, my neighbor. He owes me 800 roubles."

In general, the Azeris had plenty of canned food and bread, and the Armenians had cognac and vodka with which to barter[47], and, after the capture of the Sarsang generating plant in February 1993, electricity, which they were willing to sell to Azeri-held areas for an hour or for a day, or to withhold at will. Until the following July, when the city fell to Karabagh forces, Aghdam obtained some of its electrical power by trading with the enemy in this uncertain fashion.

Neither side was equipped to maintain prisoner-of-war camps or, as far as starving Armenians were concerned, to feed prisoners, so prisoner exchange was common. When the fortune of war turned against them, Azeri troops drove down to Baku and rounded up any surviving Armenians they could find to exchange or sell to the *Karabaghtsi*, until the Armenians decided that this trade in hostages was not to their advantage.

Prisoners and hostages were often repatriated minus any gold teeth they once had, and even enemy dead were exhumed for post-mortem dental work. Both sides revived the First World War practice of collecting the ears of enemy dead as trophies.

# MATÉRIEL

With the exception of an MP40 submachine gun that an Armenian veteran brought home from Berlin in 1945, some sporting guns, a few long guns and pistols secretly crafted in the back room of the furniture factory in Stepanakert, and the Japanese Alinco radios used by Karabagh forces, all the military hardware used in the Nagorno-Karabagh War was of Soviet origin.

Some of the home-made or field-expedient firearms can be seen in the Stepanakert Museum, but it has not been possible to substantiate stories that in desperate, bloody battles in the summer of 1992 when Azeri troops poured into Nagorno-Karabagh, even crossbows[48] and hunting knives were put to murderous use.

During the Cold War, the Soviet regime had identified Armenia as a front-line area and likely battlefield, because any real war with the West would involve Turkey, an effective and well-armed member of NATO. The de facto Turkish frontier, which Armenia does not recognize, is only a dozen miles south of Yerevan, and Mount Ararat, which dominates Yerevan's southern skyline, lies within Turkey, as a permanent reminder of the proximity of Turkish power.

Soviet military planners, therefore, based only three divisions of their 7th Guards Army in Armenia, exposed to a preemptive first strike by NATO; and there were no military airfields of any importance in the Armenian SSR.[49]

Azerbaijan was seen as a more secure area, where four divisions of the Soviet 4th Combined Arms Army could safely be based. And there were five military airfields in Azerbaijan of operational and logistical importance.

As the USSR disintegrated at the end of the 1980s, the old Soviet Union was awash with surplus military equipment, but its distribution was uneven and, for most of the duration of the war in Nagorno-Karabagh, Azerbaijan had the lion's share.

According to Tom de Waal, Armenia had just 500 railroad carloads of ammunition stored in its bunkers, while there were 10,000 ammunition wagons in Azerbaijan.[50]

A substantial part of the "orphaned" stocks of matériel sooner or later found its way into the hands of the combatants in Nagorno-Karabagh.

In the case of Azerbaijan, according to Dr. Leila Yunusova, a deputy defense minister, a nation-wide fund-raising drive helped provide funds for purchase of munitions from whoever held the keys to the vehicle parks and bunkers.

While Armenians, and particularly the *Dashnaktsutiun* and other *Diaspora* organizations, worked hard to equip their forces, they were never able to match the wholesale transfer of 4th Army weapons to Azerbaijan.

Apart from some of the equipment of the Soviet MVD garrison and of the 366th Motor Rifle Regiment based in Stepanakert, very little matériel fell into the hands of the Armenians of Nagorno-Karabagh in the early days of the campaign. At the outset, the Karabagh *fedayner* fought with only rudimentary weapons against Azeris who never experienced any shortage of arms and ammunition, up to and including T-72 tanks and *Grad* missile launchers.

The T-72s left in Stepanakert by the 366th Motor Rifle Regiment were the only main battle tanks available to Nagorno-Karabagh in the early phases of the war, although others were captured from Azeri forces later in the campaign. The Karabagh forces took particular care to capture rather than destroy vulnerable Azeri tanks as the government paid bounties for the capture of any T-72 that could be repaired and put back into service against its previous owners.

Whenever possible, anti-tank squads would aim for the tracks of Azeri T-72s, to immobilize them without doing serious damage to the hulls which housed hard-to-repair electronic systems.

The rebuilding of these battle-damaged T-72s in the Stepanakert workshops, often with parts cannibalized from more badly damaged tanks, played a vital part in equipping the armored forces of the Nagorno-Karabagh Republic.

It was on 22 December 1991, a couple of days before the Soviet Empire officially collapsed, that armed *Karabaghtsi* broke into the compound of the MVD regiment in Stepanakert and helped themselves to weapons, ammunition and armored vehicles. The now-disarmed MVD men were invited to leave Nagorno-Karabagh.

At least that was the official story. Another version has it that a business deal had been struck involving roubles and *tutovka*, the high-octane mulberry vodka for which Nagorno-Karabagh is famous. At least the MVD men would have something useful to take home with them.

Until the Lachin Corridor was forced open on 18 May 1992, the Armenians faced enormous difficulties in getting equipment and supplies into Nagorno-Karabagh.

Until the capture of the Khodjali airstrip in February 1992, all supplies had to be brought from, and the seriously wounded evacuated to Yerevan, 130 miles across the mountains, by helicopters. These choppers had to land and take off under fire from the Azeri missile and gun batteries surrounding Stepanakert.

Even after Karabagh forces captured the firebase[51] at Khodjali on 26 February, and opened a road to the outside world on 18 May, the significance of these developments was not felt immediately. The airstrip was short, planes scarce, and the Republic of Armenia was not *de jure* at war with Azerbaijan. A major airlift of arms was neither feasible nor politically prudent in the late spring of 1992, even if such arms had been available in desperately poor Armenia.

As for the road to the frontier at Lachin, it was barely drivable, for Azerbaijan had systematically neglected the infrastructure of the Nagorno-Karabagh *oblast*, and most especially the road that led to Armenia. It would be weeks before it was able to carry a significant volume of supplies to beleaguered Karabagh.

◆    ◆    ◆

The 23,000-strong Soviet 7th Guards Army was based in Armenia, and large parts of two of its three divisions, the 15th and 164th, were transferred to Armenian command under the terms of the Tashkent Treaty on Collective Security of 15 May 1992.[52] The third of the army's motor rifle divisions, the 261st, remained under Russian command at Gyumri, although it was estimated that about 25 per cent of its officers and 75 per cent of its enlisted men were actually Armenian.[53]

Under the Tashkent Treaty, Armenia was allocated 180 T-72 tanks, 180 BMP-1K tracked armored personnel carriers (APCs), 60 BTR-60 and BTR-70 wheeled APCs, 25 BRM-1K armored reconnaissance vehicles, 30 9P-138 and 9P-148 anti-tank guided missile systems (usually mounted on BRDM-2 platforms) and 130 guns and mortars.

The Soviet 4th Combined Arms Army was headquartered in Baku, with its 31st Division at Gandža, 6th at Lenkoran on the Iranian border, 75th in Nakhichevan, and 216th near Baku. In violation of the traditional Soviet policy of stationing non-Russian conscripts far from their homelands, by 1991 the 31st Guards Motor Rifle Division, as noted above, was strongly Azeri.[54]

The Tashkent Treaty had allocated a fair share of ex-Soviet matériel to Armenia on paper, but the Soviet 7th Guards Army headquartered at Gyumri, had not disintegrated as had the 4th Army.[55] It was this disintegration that loosed a flood of munitions into Azerbaijan, over and above supplies allocated at Tashkent.

But not much ex-Soviet equipment reached the Karabagh forces in the early days of the campaign, except for that abandoned by the 366th Regiment, which was actually an element of the 4th Army's 31st Division.

Although Azerbaijan was not at that time a member of the Confederation of Independent States (CIS)[56], the Tashkent Treaty allocated the divisional equipment of the 31st to Azerbaijan, including 150 tanks (mostly T-72s), 290 BMP-1 and-2 tracked APCs, 150 mortars and 90 anti-aircraft guns.

Soviet Air Force equipment was also transferred to Azerbaijan, including a squadron of Sukhoi Su-25 ground-attack aircraft (NATO codename Frogfoot).

Azeri sources report massive transfers of Russian aircraft, including MiG-29s (NATO codename Fulcrum), to Armenia, but these played no part in the Nagorno-Karabagh War, if they even existed.

Both sides acquired *Strela* (SA-7/14), Osa (SA-8), *Igla* (SA-16/18) and 23mm Shilka anti-aircraft weapons, and the Azeris also used Alazan rockets during the bombardment of Stepanakert.

The Alazan was conceived as a meteorological research tool, and was used for cloud-seeding in times of drought. Although not particularly accurate when deployed as a weapon, the Azeris found that it was effective when used against towns or villages.

Some of these Alazan rockets, equipped with nuclear warheads for some reason that is not immediately apparent, were warehoused in the early 1990s in the ex-Soviet weapons depository at Tiraspol in Transnistria, but were subsequently mislaid.

Although Col. Iskander Hamidov, the *Bozkurt* leader who was at that time minister of the interior in the Elchibey government, claimed in December 1992 that Azerbaijan had nuclear weapons, no evidence has so far appeared to indicate that the Tiraspol warheads, or any other nukes, found their way to Baku. On the other hand, the warheads haven't been credibly reported anywhere else.

After the departure of Pavel Grachev from the Russian ministry of defense in October 1996, it was revealed that 85 T-72s and 50 BMP-2 tracked infantry fighting vehicles, and other equipment to the value of $50 million, had been transferred to the Armenian army between the 1994 cease-fire and 1996.

This new hardware was delivered too late to affect the outcome of the Nagorno-Karabagh campaign, but it certainly strengthened Armenia's hand and reduced the danger of a new Azeri onslaught. This was exactly what the Russians intended.

◆    ◆    ◆

During the Karabagh War, uniforms were usually ex-Soviet, but particularly among the *fedayner*, a uniform was whatever durable clothing one owned. Consequently, uniforms were anything but uniform.

The most commonly worn garments were components of the Soviet M1982 *afghanka* series of field uniforms, which consisted of pants, jacket and headgear. These had evolved into a very practicable system during the Afghanistan campaign.[57]

The *afghanka* jacket was well-provided with pockets, including characteristic pockets on the upper arms.

Initially the *afghanka* series consisted of tan or khaki summer and winter-weight garments, but later in the Afghan campaign, camouflaged versions, similar to the British Disruptive Pattern Material (DPM) and the American Woodland designs, started to appear. As it was only in the mid-1990s that the Russian Federation started to adopt exotic and digital camouflage patterns, no *Pyatnisto-fioletovoye* (spotted violet), *Ten'* (shadow) or *Tigr* (tiger) uniforms were seen during the war.

During the winter campaigns, the synthetic fleece collars of the winter-weight *afghanka* were much appreciated, and a lucky few acquired *shuba* or *obchina* sheepskin coats.

The blue and white striped undershirt, the *telniyashka* if sleeveless, or *maika* with sleeves, originally a uniform item of the Tsarist fleet, spread at the behest of Maj.Gen. Vasiliy F. Margelov from the naval infantry in which he made his reputation (although an army major), to the VDV (*Vozdushno-Desantnaya Voyska*) or airborne forces, which he came to command in 1956.

By the time of the Karabagh War, one or other version of the undershirt was worn by individuals who had no claim to membership of any elite unit.

Some Karabagh units wore distinctive badges, for example the *Dashnak* companies wore a badge incorporating the red flag of revolution and the crossed pen, spade and sword.

During the storming of Shoushi, Karabagh troops adorned their uniforms, equipment and tanks with white crosses, less out of crusading zeal than to avoid casualties from friendly fire in an environment in which everyone was dressed and equipped more or less the same.

In subsequent actions, Azeri troops painted the star and crescent motif, the *ay yildiz* of the Azerbaijan flag, on their tanks and cannon barrels, and the men of Surat Husseinov's 709th Brigade identified their tanks with a boldly-lettered SURAT on the turret.

### CIS Treaty on Collective Security, 15 May 1992

| | ARMENIA | AZERBAIJAN* | ACTUAL AZ.**<br>(May 1992) |
|---|---|---|---|
| Main battle tanks (T-72) | 180 | 150 (non-<br>specif.) | 286 |
| BMP-1 and-2 armored personnel carriers | 180) | | |
| BTR-60/70 armored personnel carriers | 60) | 290 | 842 |
| BRM-1K armored fighting vehicles | 25) | | |
| 9P-138/148 guided a/t missile systems | 30 | | |
| *Grad*/Hail BM-21 system | ? | | ? |
| Field artillery | 130 | | 386 |
| Anti-aircraft artillery | | 90 | |
| Mortars | | 150 | |
| MANPADs *** | | | |
| Marine | | | Part of Caspian<br>Flotilla |
| Aviation | | | Squadron of<br>Sukhoi Su-25s<br>At least 4 Mi-24<br>gunships |

\* Azerbaijan did not formally join the CIS until Sept. 1993, but at Tashkent was allocated much of the equipment of the 4th Army's motor rifle divisions.

\*\* Statement by Azeri Foreign Ministry, Nov. 1993, quoted by Dmitry Danilov in "Russia's Search for International Mandate" (Coppetiers' *Contested Borders in the Caucasus,* note 161).

\*\*\* Man-Portable Air Defense System (MANPADS) Designations:

| US Military desig. for surface-air missiles | NATO Air Standardization Coordinating Cttee. reporting name | Russian Military designation for missile system | Comparable US system |
| --- | --- | --- | --- |
| SA-7 | Grail | 9K32 *Strela*-2 | Redeye |
| SA-9 | Gaskin | 9K31 *Strela*-1 | |
| SA-13 | Gopher | 9K35 *Strela*-10 | |
| SA-14 | Gremlin | 9K34 *Strela*-3 | |
| SA-16 | Gimlet | 9K310 *Igla*-1 | Stinger |
| SA-18 | Grouse | 9K38 *Igla* | |

# STRATEGIC OBJECTIVES

Shortly before he died in 1989, Nobel Peace Prize laureate Andrei Sakharov wrote that "the Armenian people are again facing the threat of genocide … for Nagorno-Karabakh this is a question of survival, for Azerbaijan—just a question of ambition".

That ambition, for at least some Azeris, was to reach out across Nagorno-Karabagh, across Armenia's southern Syunik province, and the isolated Azeri autonomous republic of Nakhichevan[58], toward Turkey, with a view to creating the western arm of *Turan*, the pan-Turkic empire that Turkish nationalists had long dreamed of.

Creation of *Turan* was the primary goal of the Turkish and Azeri branches of the Nationalist Action Party, otherwise known as the Gray Wolves. *Bozkurt*, the Gray Wolf, is a guiding, talismanic figure in Turkic mythology, and the eastern arm of *Turan* would include the Turkic peoples of Central Asia whence the Grey Wolf came. So *Bozkurt* is a concept of some geostrategic significance, either as a vehicle for Islamic fundamentalism, or as a bulwark against it.

Sakharov may not have been totally objective where Karabagh was concerned, although it is hard to fault his analysis. The family of his second wife, Elena Bonner[59], was Armenian and originally came from Shoushi. Her father, Gevork Alikhanov or Alikhanian, started his political career with the *Dashnaks* but later transferred his allegiance to the Bolsheviks, and it was Alikhanov who proclaimed the Red victory in Yerevan. He was a senior official of the Comintern in 1937 when he and many of his colleagues fell victim to Nikolai Ivanovich Yezhov's pursuit of Stalin's real and imagined enemies.[60]

The Azeris made no secret of their plans for Nagorno-Karabagh. On assuming power in Baku in June 1992, Abulfaz Elchibey said, "If there is a single Armenian left in Karabagh this October, Azeris will hang him in Baku's Central Square."

Given the pattern of relations between the two ethnic groups over the years, Armenians tended to believe he meant what he said. If *Operation Koltso*, Baku's ethnic-cleansing campaign in the Spring of 1991, hadn't made the point, Elchibey certainly did a year later.

Ever since the creation of the *oblast* in 1923, the Baku leadership recognized that isolating the Armenians of Nagorno-Karabagh was the key to suppressing Armenian resistance there.

There was little industry in Nagorno-Karabagh. No oil or strategically important minerals were being exploited. There was nothing but the modest hydro-electric plant below the Sarsang Reservoir. So when the Soviet Union crumbled and matters came to a head, centers of population and communication hubs tended to be the focus of Azeri military activity.

In October 1990, Azeri troops occupied Khodjali, site of Nagorno-Karabagh's only airfield, and turned it into a well-fortified firebase from which they could bombard Stepanakert, a few miles to the south and, at the same time, control the only highway between the capital and the Armenian communities in northern Karabagh. This road runs along the airfield's eastern perimeter fence.

As one of the most menacing of the Azeri firebases that surrounded Stepanakert, Khodjali became an early objective of the *Karabaghtsi*, but the importance of the airfield and firebase were as obvious to the Baku leadership as to the Armenians.

To strengthen their position there, the Azeris settled a community of Meskhetian Turks at Khodjali. These Meskhetians were descendants of Ottoman Turks who had settled in Meskheti, an area just north of the Ottoman Empire's border with Georgia. Fearing that Turkey might enter the Second World War on the Axis side, Stalin deported 47,000 of these people to the deserts of south-eastern Uzbekistan, where they would pose no threat. And there they remained for half a century, hoping always that they would eventually be allowed to return to their homes in the green valleys of the southern Caucasus.

The collapse of the Soviet Union, and Uzbekistan's declaration of independence in August 1991, left them in limbo, no longer Soviet citizens, hardly Uzbeks, and as far as ever from Georgia. When their fellow Moslems in Azerbaijan offered them homes in Nagorno-Karabagh, many came. It seemed at least a step closer to Meskheti, although they may have realized that they were being used as pawns in a dangerous game.

The most dangerous of the other firebases that ringed Stepanakert was on the cliff-wall of the ancient town of Shoushi a few miles to the south. Shoushi's guns and missile launchers also commanded the road from Stepanakert south to Lachin, so that the Nagorno-Karabagh capital was pinned between two Azeri strong-points.

As the Azeris considered the old and once cosmopolitan town of Shoushi to be their ancient capital and had underlined the point by massacring hundreds of the town's Armenian inhabitants in March 1920, who held Shoushi was a matter of more than military importance.

◆    ◆    ◆

So it was that in the last months of the Soviet regime, the Armenians of Nagorno-Karabagh had no airport and no surface link with the Republic of Armenia, nor with any other possible source of aid. Their only link with the outside world was by helicopter. As Stepanakert came under heavy bombardment in September 1991, even this link became tenuous.

If they were to survive, the *Karabaghtsi* had to break the Azeri stranglehold and open air and land communication with the outside world.

Control over the airfield, and the land route through the Lachin Corridor to Armenia and the rest of the world, across the six-mile strip of Azerbaijan that Stalin had placed in the way, were vital.. However, seizing them would not solve Nagorno-Karabagh's problems as long as the Azeris continued to pound Stepanakert and the towns and villages of Nagorno-Karabagh from their ring of firebases.

Diplomacy was not an option in the context of ethnic cleansing, and appeasement would be suicide.

If the *Karabaghtsi* were to survive, their solution had to be a military one. The solution that the Armenians of Nagorno-Karabagh found to their problem had its origin in the last days of the Soviet regime.

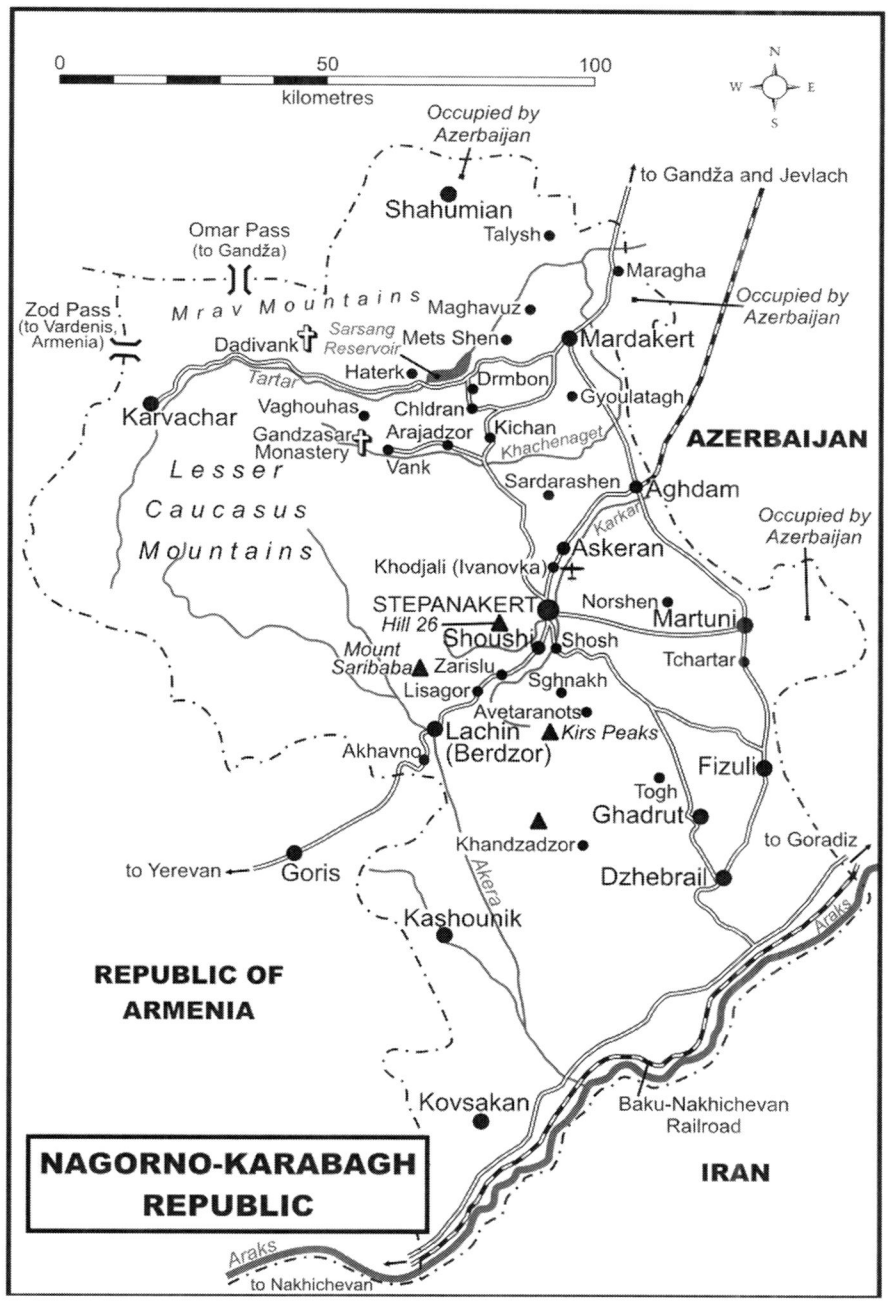

Ruins of an apartment building in Stepanakert hit by a 500kg bomb dropped by an Azeri Sukhoi Su-25 ground-attack aircraft. Most people who lived here had taken refuge in underground shelters, but the wife of a soldier and his two small daughters were killed in this incident. The husband, serving at the front, had to be restrained from killing himself when told that his whole family had been wiped out.

Burying a fallen comrade. Funeral of Commander Sergei Tovmassyan, whose brother was also killed in battle.

Waiting to ambush the Azeri gunships. A father and son Strela-2 team, armed with the anti-aircraft missile that NATO calls the SA-7 Grail. It was fired from a disposable tube mounted on a reusable gripstock.

One of the improvised pistols manufactured in the back room of a furniture factory in Stepanakert early in the war (Stepanakert Museum).

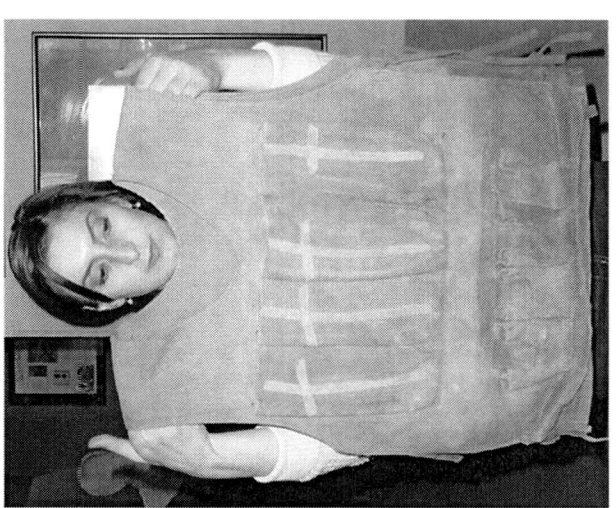

As both Karabaghtsi and Azeris wore the same Soviet kit, the Karabaghtsi often identified themselves and their tanks with white crosses. Gayane of the Stepanakert Museum displays a canvas magazine/grenade vest.

Battlefield nurse Aida Seropian, a decorated hero-mother of Karabagh.

Pavlik Manochian's Dashnak comrades considered him a bit of a show-off, as most of them went to war in boring old afghanka uniforms or bits and pieces thereof, but his adoption of the traditional Karabagh costume was entirely consistent with the strongly nationalist tradition of the fedayn, and parallels the fedayn dress of the 1890s and of Dashnak resistance fighters during the genocide years of the First World War. He wears the traditional kinjal hanging from his belt. His folding-stock AKM and the 7.62mm cartridges in his bandoliers are his only concessions to modernity.

Arkadi Ter Tadevosian, victor of Shoushi

Seyran Ohanian as a Soviet Army major

Ashot 'Oskolka' Ghulian. Oskolka means fragmentation in Russian. His body was full of bits of grenade

Youra Hovhanissian

Proud mother sends her son off to the war.

Karabagh azatamartic (freedom-fighter) brings in an Azeri prisoner, who will be ransomed or exchanged minus his army boots, which appear much superior to the light civilian shoes his captor wears.

Love blooms amid the carnage.

Three types of the Karabagh army.

Kristofor Ivanian had been one of Zhukov's artillery commanders during the Great Patriotic War. Aged 72, he was quietly dying of cancer in St.Petersburg when he heard that Karabagh was in trouble. He came south and, with Stalinist discipline, licked the officer corps of the Karabagh army into war-winning shape. In this photograph, he is wearing a strichtarn camouflage field jacket, East German army issue from 1965 to 1990.

Vagho Beglarian was an MVD officer in the North Caucasus when the Soviet Empire collapsed. When his home town of Mardakert was threatened, he came south to join the Karabagh forces, leaving his wife and family safe in Chechnya. His wife and daughter were killed in what became the hell of Grozny, but Vagho survived three years of ferocious see-saw fighting, finishing the war as a highly-decorated lieutenant colonel in the Karabagh army.

Karabagh tankers with their mascot Blackie.

Dismounted one-piece cast turret and 125mm smoothbore gun of an Azeri T-72, destroyed during the defence of Aghdam in July 1993. The "bricks" of Kontakt-5 explosive reactive armour (ERA) demonstrably proved inadequate in this case. Although Karabagh forces made every effort to capture Azeri T-72s intact so they could be reflagged and put back into action against their previous owners, penetration of the poorly-armoured hulls by an anti-tank round usually caused the ammunition supply to detonate and blow off the turret; shells and diesel fuel were packed together.

Karabagh rifleman covers advancing comrades during the battle for the Aghdam railhead which was captured 23-24 July 1993. He is armed with the 5.45mm AK-74, although the 7.62mm AKM was also widely used.

Defensive position near Mardakert, spring 1993. In addition to the belt-fed 7.62mm PK general purpose machine gun, the Karabagh soldier has an old but effective RPG-7 ready for use. He wears a camouflaged winter-weight afghanka jacket, as nights can be cold on the Tartar steppe.

This Karabagh soldier, pictured near the wreckage of battle not far from Drmbon in March 1993, is armed with a 7.62mm AKM rifle with extended 45-round magazine and grenade launcher. He wears a winter-weight afghanka jacket over the blue-and-white-striped maika, originally worn by the Tsarist navy, then by special forces, but by this time generally worn by Karabagh troops. The black ribbon tied around his right arm is in mourning for fallen comrades, as Karabagh casualties were heavy in the fighting for the Sarsang Reservoir and hydro-electric plant.

Monte Melkonian—California-born archeologist and freedom-fighter, killed in action on the Aghdam front in June 1993.

Helmets were not often worn during the Karabagh War, but had other uses, as fighting is thirsty work.

Supreme Catolicos Vasken I Baljian (1908–94) blesses Karabagh troops.

# MILITARY OPERATIONS

## OPENING MOVES (TO DECEMBER 1991)

In February 1988, reacting to rumors of intercommunal trouble in Chardakhlu in Azerbaijan, and in the Kapan region of Armenia, Azeri mobs attacked and killed Armenians in Sumgait, a drab Communist-era industrial city of 250,000, 20 miles north of Baku, and subsequently in Baku and in other parts of Azerbaijan.

As refugees from the *pogroms* poured into their *oblast*, the Armenians of Nagorno-Karabagh realized more than ever that their survival depended on their homeland being united with the rest of Armenia or, at least, independent of Azerbaijan.

The Nagorno-Karabagh *oblast* soviet voted to secede from Azerbaijan on 12 July 1988. The decision was vetoed immediately by the Azerbaijan supreme soviet. Over the next few months the people of Nagorno-Karabagh, reinforced by Armenian refugees who continued to stream in from more vulnerable parts of Azerbaijan, started to arm themselves and form self-defense units.

In September 1988, following confrontations between refugees from Sumgait and Azeri residents of Nagorno-Karabagh, Moscow imposed martial law, but tension increased in December with news of more anti-Armenian *pogroms* in Azerbaijan and a new flood of refugees.

Why the Azeris suddenly decided to attack their Armenian neighbors after seventy years of Moscow-imposed peace is still unclear. Certainly there were latent tensions, but also a two or three generation tradition of cooperation within the Communist Party, and on a commercial and even social level. Mixed marriages were not unheard of. But once the first attacks took place, retaliation and escalation quickly followed.

Conspiracy theorists blame Mikhail Sergeyevich Gorbachev, whose apparently benign reforms were running into trouble by the late 1980s. Many in the monolithic Soviet security establishment feared that his policies would lead to a meltdown—a catastrophic loss of central government power—and pressed Gorbachev to endorse a *konspiratsia* to purge such centrifugal groups as the Azerbaijani Popular Front, founded in March 1989, with Abulfaz Elchibey emerging as party chairman the following July.

The nationalist APF was violently opposed to self-determination for Nagorno-Karabagh. That was one thing Moscow and the APF agreed on.

Rail traffic between Azerbaijan and Armenia was interrupted by the Azeris in the summer of 1989 as the APF flexed its muscles. In August, Azerbaijan started to enforce an economic blockade of Armenia and Nagorno-Karabagh. In November railroad traffic between Azerbaijan and the Armenian territories ceased altogether.

Later that month, the Moscow supreme soviet voted to "normalize" the situation in Nagorno-Karabagh by imposing tighter Soviet control.

A few days later, the Yerevan supreme soviet and the *oblast* soviet of Nagorno-Karabagh passed a joint resolution "on reunification of the Soviet Socialist Republic of Armenia and Nagorno-Karabagh". The Baku supreme soviet rejected the resolution.

Following further anti-Armenian *pogroms* in Baku in "Black January" of 1990, Soviet paratroopers entered the city, and about 17,000 additional Soviet MVD troops were sent to Nagorno-Karabagh, to reinforce the

Azeri OMON already deployed there, establishing checkpoints on key roads to limit movement of Armenians. In response to the violence in Baku, a state of emergency had been proclaimed 200 miles away in Nagorno-Karabagh, but not actually in Baku.

In Russia, the OMON *Black Berets* are the MVD's special forces.[61] The term was picked up by the Azerbaijan government for its 10,000-strong auxiliary police, largely recruited from Azeris who had fled Armenia at the beginning of the trouble over Nagorno-Karabagh. Many of them saw service in OMON as an opportunity to settle old scores.

In Baku, more than a hundred Azeris were killed fighting the Soviet paratroopers who had been called in too late to head off trouble, and a state of emergency was finally declared there and in other parts of Azerbaijan.[62]

Some of the circumstances surrounding the belated use in Baku in January 1990 of the airborne forces commanded by Lt.Gen. Aleksandr Ivanovich Lebed, lend credibility to anti-Gorbachev theories.

Lebed's paratroopers were fighting their way into Baku, when a high-powered team of military lawyers arrived from Moscow intent on scapegoating Lebed on charges of excessive brutality. According to the American Lt.Gen. William E. Odom[63], Lebed withdrew the lawyers' protective detail and they were forthwith pinned down by APF gunfire.

Lebed only agreed to rescue them when the Russian judge advocate general admitted that the charges against the paratroop commander were fabricated and totally groundless, having been drawn up by the Gorbachev administration in Moscow before the paras had even reached Baku, with the intent of neutralizing Lebed, whose political ambitions were no secret. The plan had been to kill two birds with one stone: Lebed would destroy the APF, and be destroyed himself in the process.

In fact, Lebed would place third in the 1996 Russian presidential election, having commanded the Russian 14th Guards Army in Tiraspol, safely out of the mainstream of Russian politics, from 1992 to 1995. To the relief of many in the Russian political establishment, he died in a helicopter crash in 2002 at the age of fifty-two.

◆    ◆    ◆

And Armenia too was arming, much to Moscow's alarm. On 25 July 1990, Gorbachev prohibited creation of any armed formations not under Moscow control. Specific targets were the two Yerevan militias: Azgaldian's AAI, and the ANA led by Vasilian and Vartanian.

Combined, the two organizations probably had no more than 2,500 members, but had been fairly successful in obtaining weapons from Armenians in the Soviet armed forces.

Levon Ter-Petrosian[64], elected chairman of the Armenian supreme soviet in August 1990, and de facto ruler of Armenia, used fighting between ANA troops and Azeris on the frontier north of Nagorno-Karabagh as an excuse to bring the militias to heel. He disbanded the ANA, and the AAI turned itself into a political party. In September 1991, 2,000 AAI fighters were formally mustered into OMOR, interior ministry forces of the newly independent Armenian Republic.

Despite a heavy Soviet presence, the Armenians of Nagorno-Karabagh realized increasingly that war was inevitable. They renewed their efforts to create an effective self-defense force.

Ter-Petrosian's interior minister, Ashot Manucharian, was one of those who helped the Karabagh resistance fighters to obtain weapons from Soviet army units in Georgia. As there was no possibility of transporting anything but infantry weapons into Karabagh, these were usually small arms, rocket-propelled grenades, and a few 82 mm mortars.

During the guerrilla war that soon developed in Karabagh, the Armenians were heavily outnumbered and outgunned. They weren't winning, but as long as they continued to fight, they would not lose. And they did continue to fight.

In 1991, the Soviet Union's last year of existence, loyalties were tested. Many Armenian soldiers and MVD men turned over their weapons to the *fedayner*, and many who were based in other parts of the Soviet Union, came home to join the resistance.

Vagho Beglarian was a Soviet MVD officer in Grozny, the Chechen capital. He came south to join the *fedayner* in his home town of Mardakert, leaving his wife and family safe in Chechnya. He survived three years of savage see-saw fighting on the northern and eastern frontiers of Nagorno-Karabagh, finishing the war as a highly-decorated lieutenant-colonel in the Nagorno-Karabagh army. But 250 miles north, in what became the hell of Grozny, his wife was killed and his daughter mortally wounded. His son would spend years in hospital in Yerevan.

In January 1991, saying they were just checking *propiskas*[65], the Baku government launched an ethnic-cleansing operation in Nagorno-Karabagh, called *Operation Koltso*. Azeri and Soviet OMON special forces, supported by soldiers of the largely Azeri 31st Motor Rifle Division from Gandža, raided twenty-four villages in Nagorno-Karabagh. The Armenian inhabitants were rounded up and deported to the frontier of the Republic of Armenia. The homes they had left were looted and destroyed, either by the troops or by the horde of Azeri civilians that followed them in convoys of trucks, to strip the villages clean.

"Azerification" was the underlying objective. Armenians were less likely to return if they had nothing to come back to. In some cases, Azeris who had earlier fled the Kapan region of Armenia were resettled in abandoned homes.

In Russian, *koltso* means ring. The Baku interior ministry's choice of that name for the ethnic-cleansing operation resonated in ex-Soviet communities because an earlier *Operation Koltso* had been studied obsessively in every Soviet school for almost half a century. It was during this first *Operation Koltso* in January 1943, that Stalin's armies had strangled the German 6$^{th}$ Army to death at Stalingrad.

Nor was it surprising that internal security forces should use the army term, for NKVD infantry had fought at Stalingrad. The 10$^{th}$ NKVD Rifle Division, for example, headed the order of battle of Chuikov's 62$^{nd}$ Army. The NKVD, the *Narodnyi Komissariat Vnutrennikh Del* (People's Commissariat for Internal Affairs) became the KGB in 1954.

In February 1991, while the ashes of Armenian homes in Karabagh still smouldered, the Armenian supreme soviet in Yerevan declared Stalin's original 1921 decision to give Nagorno-Karabagh to Azerbaijan to be illegal.

The Nagorno-Karabagh Republic (NKR) was proclaimed on 2 September 1991, to include the Armenian-inhabited territory of Shahumian which had not been part of the Nagorno-Karabagh *oblast.*. Stepanakert was to be the national capital and a "self-defense force" of about 15,000 would be under the control of a Committee of Defense. Leonard Petrosian was elected Chairman of the NKR's Executive Committee.

A fortnight later, the Republic of Armenia voted for independence from USSR, with Levon Ter-Petrosian as president.

In October and November 1991, Nagorno-Karabagh *azatamartics,* or freedom fighters, liberated most of the villages in the Martuni and Ghadrut regions that had been taken by the Azeris during *Operation Koltso,* although they were very short of weapons and matériel.

Progress toward building the self-defense force was slow. By the end of 1991, only a dozen units had been established in Nagorno-Karabagh, many armed only with hunting rifles or improvised weapons.

# SHOUSHI AND THE LACHIN CORRIDOR (JANUARY TO MAY 1992)

Although Stepanakert was chosen as the capital of the Nagorno-Karabagh Republic, Shoushi, ancient, walled capital of Karabagh, half a dozen miles to the south, was particularly dear to the hearts of both Armenians and Azeris.

Stepanakert stands above the left bank of the River Karkar, not far below the place where the waters of the Vararakn, flowing swiftly down from the western hills, meet those of the Karintak river, which rises to the south. Shoushi stands on a high plateau between these two streams, with the Karintak flowing close under the cliff on which the town's eastern wall is built.

Shoushi dates back to the Persian era, but the site was valued and occupied for its defensible and strategic merits since the earliest human occupation of these mountains.[66] Both Christians and Moslems lived here, often quite amicably, as they did in many towns and villages in the Caucasus, so the massacre of Armenians here in March 1920 came as a surprise to many.

The collapse of the Ottoman and Russian Empires at the end of the First World War, and the power struggle that followed, among Bolsheviks, *Müsavatist* Tartars[67], and British and German agents, resulted in great instability in the Caucasus frontier region.

The arrival of Tartar troops on 23 March 1920 signaled the beginning of a bloodbath that converted polyglot Shoushi into an Azeri stronghold.

The account of one witness, a 16-year-old Armenian youth named Suren, goes far to explain the subsequent history of Nagorno-Karabagh. He hid under a staircase in the yard of his family's house when the Tartars attacked, shooting his engineer father and a brother. They stripped, raped and then killed his mother. Then her two young sons were raped and murdered. Then her virgin daughter was subjected to every kind of bestiality before being bayoneted to death. Finally, a big Tartar *asker*[68] smashed the head of the family's three-year-old daughter, Anahit, against a wall as if it were a ripe melon.

Why? She had cried as she saw her family massacred.

Suren watched it all, shaking with fear. Grieving most of all for his baby sister, he finally crept away to join the Armenian *fedayn* militia, to inflict much the same sort of treatment on Tartars who fell into his hands, until A.I. Gekker's 11th Red Army imposed Soviet rule on Karabagh in May 1920, and brought peace again.

It would be nice to think that the Armenians forgave and forgot what happened at Shoushi, but the walls of the old town stood proud at the southern end of the Stepanakert valley as a permanent reminder of homes and loved ones that were lost.

So it was that in the autumn of 1991, Shoushi was an Azeri town and the main firebase from which Azeri gunners poured shells and missiles into Stepanakert.

On 25 September, the bombardment began in earnest. Not only Shoushi, but nearby Azeri villages were turned into firebases so that Stepanakert could be hammered from all directions until there were no more Armenians left to threaten the territorial integrity of Azerbaijan.

From December, batteries of BM-21/*Grad* missiles were used to bombard Stepanakert, as well as modified Alazan meteorological rockets.

Shells and missiles rained down from the north. The airport at Khodjali, seized by the Azeris in October 1990, was now a firebase garrisoned by OMON troops under the command of Alif Hajiev.

Lack of an airport was a serious problem for Karabagh. As the Nagorno-Karabakh *oblast* was entirely surrounded by Azeri territory, its land borders were easily sealed. The only supplies that came in, and the only casualties that were evacuated, were carried by Armenian helicopters, under the muzzles of the Azeri anti-aircraft guns and a miscellany of man-portable air-defense systems (MANPADS) like the *Strela* and the *Igla*.

Throughout the winter months, the citizens of Stepanakert froze and starved in basements, bunkers and holes in the ground as the bombardment went on day and night. Water had to be carried in buckets from a few wells on the edge of town. Stocks of antiseptics and other medical supplies were soon exhausted. It was hard even to bury the dead in the frozen ground.

On 26 January 1992, Azerbaijan's defense minister, a former Soviet staff officer named Tajedin Mekhtiev, led an attack on the Armenian village of Karintak, south of Shoushi. *Fedayner* ambushed and routed the Azeri raiders, killing as many as ninety of them. Mekhtiev was recalled to Baku where Azerbaijan's first post-Soviet president, Ayaz Mutalibov, fired him from his cabinet post.

The same month, a joint force of Karabagh and ex-Soviet 366th Motor Rifle Regiment troops neutralized Azeri OMON positions around Karkijahan, southwest of Stepanakert, and in February, Azeri firebases at Malibeyli and Ghushcilar, northeast of Stepanakert, were silenced.

But later in February the Azeris took over a huge stockpile of ex-Soviet munitions in the railhead town of Aghdam, northeast of Nagorno-Karabagh, and used helicopters to supply their remaining firebases around Stepanakert. Longer-range artillery and missile batteries pounded Stepanakert from the Karabagh-Azerbaijan frontier.

Azerbaijan Popular Front leader Rahim Gaziev took more *Grad* missile launchers up to Shoushi and, with rockets airlifted in from Aghdam, opened an intensified bombardment of Stepanakert. What was left of the already shattered town was being blown to pieces. The 366th Motor Rifle Regiment now came under fire. While its cantonment at the southern end of Stepanakert was not a primary target, there were casualties, for the *Grad* is not a precision weapon.

Before the end of February, it was obvious to the *Karabaghtsi* that the fire-bases, and particularly the airfield, had to be taken before the Karabagh community was blasted off the face of the earth.

The Karabagh intelligence service reported that the time was ripe for a counter-attack. The blow fell on Khodjali on the night of 25-26 February.

Karabagh troops and two battalions of the 366th, spearheaded by the regiment's armored vehicles, attacked Khodjali, the heavily-defended firebase that commanded the road north from Stepanakert to Askeran, and was Nagorno-Karabagh's only airfield.

Accounts of what happened next are confused. Some say the Azeri OMON garrison fought to the last man; others that the Azeri troops ran faster than the Meskhetian Turk civilians they had been using as human shields.

Being short of both men and munitions for what looked like being a protracted war, the Karabagh attackers left the Khodjali garrison an escape route to Aghdam, the Azeri base ten miles north, in the hope that they could achieve their objective without too desperate a fight and the casualties that such a battle would entail. But instead of moving north along the Aghdam road, it appears that many of those evacuating Khodjali went east, across the shallow Karkar River and into the snow-covered hills around Nakhijevanik, only then turning north toward Aghdam and across the front line.

Azeris say that it was here that pursuing Karabagh and Russian soldiers massacred hundreds of Azeri civilians, including children.

The *Karabakhtsi* claim that it was the Azeri troops, defending positions in front of Aghdam, who killed the fugitives, not realizing that the people running through the night toward their lines were friends.

But they also accuse the Azeri OMON troops of murdering thirty-four Armenian prisoners at Khodjali before the attack. Just as the OMON troops defending Khodjali included Azeris who had fled from Armenia's Kapan region at the start of the war, so did the attacking Karabagh troops include refugees from the *pogroms* of Sumgait and Baku. Both sides had old scores to settle.

Apart from the obvious relief afforded the bombarded and battered citizens of Stepanakert, and the possibility of an air bridge to Armenia, the capture of Khodjali had two important outcomes. The Azeris realized that while unarmed Armenian villagers might not pose much of a problem to their OMON stalwarts, the Karabagh troops and their allies, could be quite dangerous when they took the offensive.

Secondly, negative publicity about the civilian casualties at Khodjali, collateral damage in a battle in which two Russian battalions had fought, led Moscow to order the withdrawal of the 366th Motor Rifle Regiment from Stepanakert.

Facing the OMON and the entire Azeri army, reinforced by other elements of the of Soviet 4th Army which had been based in Azerbaijan, the *Karabaghtsi* did not want the 366th to go. They blocked the withdrawal route, so that many of the Russians had to be airlifted out and others escorted by Russian *Spetsnaz* troops to Georgia, where the 366th was disbanded.

Azeri sources claim that the Russians left twenty-five tanks, eighty-seven armored fighting vehicles, twenty-eight other armored vehicles, and forty-five mortars for the Karabagh forces.

Karabagh sources put the figures at about half these totals, but the 366th did leave behind more than a hundred Armenian officers and men, including Maj. Seyran Ohanian, commander of the 2nd Battalion and a future general and minister of defense of the Nagorno-Karabagh Republic.

Another former Soviet officer who found himself in Nagorno-Karabagh at this time was Arkady Ter-Tatevosian. His *nom de guerre* was 'Komandos' and he had his eye on Shoushi. He sat down with Gurgen Daribaltayan, and army chief of staff, Felix Gzoghyan, to see what could be done.

Stepanakert was still under daily bombardment, but the *Karabaghtsi* saw that Shoushi was now vulnerable. The roles of besieger and besieged were shifting. During the winter, Stepanakert had been isolated, with nothing going for it but its citizens' resolution, fortified by the conviction that few of them would survive if the Azeris took the town.

The capture of the airfield had changed that. Stepanakert was now linked with Armenia, and through Armenia, with three million more Armenians in the *Diaspora*, and the *Karabaghtsi* were showing their teeth as one Azeri outpost after another fell. The Shoushi garrison's sense of isolation was reinforced when one of their own supply helicopters was shot down with a *Strela* shoulder-fired anti-aircraft missile[69].

Their attempts to turn the tables on increasingly aggressive Karabagh troops weren't working.

Then in a firefight waged intermittently between 23 April and 5 May at Lachin, Dnieprik Baghdassarian's Republic of Armenia gunners destroyed Azeri batteries that had, unwisely, been shelling targets inside Armenia.

The Shoushi garrison wondered what would happen next, for the only road out of Shoushi that wasn't directly controlled by the *Karabaghtsi*, wound down from the mountains and through now-defenseless Lachin. There seemed to be a real possibility that bombardment by Armenian artillery would be followed up by Armenian armor and infantry, who were massed just across the frontier.

Political considerations had forced the Yerevan government to resist pressure to come to the aid of Stepanakert, but once Azeri shells started landing on Armenian territory, it was far from certain that retaliation would be limited to Baghdassarian's counter-bombardment.

◆     ◆     ◆

Karabagh troops had captured the Azeri firebase at Hogher at the end of March, removing a threat to villages of the Ghadrut region, but Azeri forces retaliated at Maragha on Karabagh's north-eastern border on 10 April, looting and then destroying the village. In this instance, Western parliamentarians were at the scene before the headless bodies were cold, to confirm the usual atrocity stories.[70]

Maragha was another of those pointless incidents that blemish the history of inter-communal relations in Karabagh. The survivors of the village which is now on the Azeri side of the cease-fire line, were relocated at Nor Maragha on the Khachenaget River. Travelers note that years after their families were butchered like hogs, something worse than grief still scars the faces of those who had to match the sawn-off heads of loved ones to the charred bodies the Azeris left behind.

On 29-30 April, an attempt to tighten the noose that Ter-Tatevosian was drawing tight around Shoushi, resulted in a ferocious battle at Hill 26 west of the town. An Azeri counter-attack was beaten off after a close-fought battle, by Karabagh defenders led by Youra Hovhannisian, henceforth known as 'Youra of 26'.

Before closing in for the kill, Ter-Tatevosian continued to deal with the Azeri firebases around Shoushi, one after another. As soldiers say, he was preparing the battlefield.

Moreover, having too few men and too few guns and too few tanks and no air force at all, with which to take a fortress deemed impregnable, he was "messing with the heads" of the Azeris in the best PsyWar[71] tradition, subtly inviting them to follow him, step by step, to the conclusion that they were doomed.

By all available means, and especially by demonstrations of confidence, Ter-Tatevosian sought to convince the Azeris that his force was vastly stronger than it was, and moreover, that any day, Republic of Armenia troops might pour across the frontier and up the Lachin Corridor, to take Shoushi in the rear.

On 7 May, desperate Azeri troops attacked *fedayn* positions southeast of Stepanakert. Bombardment of the town with *Grad* missiles and artillery from Shoushi and Janhasan intensified once more.

The *fedayner,* led by Youra Hovhannisyan and Seyran Ohanian, struck back. They neutralized firebases on the western hills at Janhasan and Kyos-alar, capturing a *Grad* missile launcher and a large supply of ammunition, and destroying several BMP-1 and BMP-2 infantry combat vehicles.[72]

Other forces secured Shosh, east of Shoushi. It was to be one of the bases for the final attack.

The *Dashnak* battalion destined to be Shamil Basayev's nemesis, was camped in the Sghnakh Forests. It marched westward across country in two columns. One, commanded by Enver Chakhoyan, marched up the Karintak valley, while Jirayr Sefilyan's column moved due west. When they met up again at Zarislu, it was to control the road between Shoushi and Lachin. Fleeing Azeris would be given free passage and encouraged on their way. Any relief forces that might come up from the direction of Lachin would be dealt with, but it was obvious by this point that the Azeris had no means of reinforcing the garrison.

Even if troops had been on hand, Baku could not be sure, after the recent firefight, that the Republic of Armenia troops would not interfere with any attempt to save Shoushi.

Shoushi occupied a position of great tactical strength, but it was increasingly obvious in Baku that it was strategically vulnerable.

◆    ◆    ◆

Things hadn't been going well in Shoushi. Rahim Gaziev, who took over from Mekhtiev, brought in new hardware and munitions, but failed to unite the four different units nominally under his command, and was probably relieved when called back to Baku on 6 March to take over as defense minister in Yaqub K. Mamedov's interim government[73].

After his departure little was done to put the town's defenses in order. Then in April, Lt.Col. Elbrus Orujev was put in command of a newly-formed Shoushi Brigade, but given responsibility not only for Shoushi, but for Lachin, Kashounik and Kovsakan. With a full-time job in Shoushi, he was also tasked with fighting the war across most of the territory between his base and the Iranian border.

Baku's decision to use a lieutenant-colonel as both a garrison commander, a job appropriate to his rank, and as a brigade commander with wide-ranging responsibilities, might be regarded as defeatist or even desperate. Evidently senior Azeri officers were not competing for the Shoushi assignment.

The failure of the Azeri air force to play any significant role in the defense of Shoushi may also have been due to a feeling that there were no laurels to be won, and that if Azeri planes intervened, Republic of Armenia pilots might also join in, provoking war on a scale that no one wanted.

Shoushi's Azeri defenders started to disappear. Orujev, his telephone communications cut in early May by advancing *fedayner*, broadcast a radio appeal for help. His brother Elkhan, commanding troops in Aghdam, launched an attack toward Stepanakert, but too little and too late to help Shoushi.

H-hour was 2:30 am on 8 May 1992. Ter-Tatevosian was sufficiently encouraged by what his spies and scouts told him to disregard the principles of war and divide his command in the face of an enemy whose forces, at the beginning of the action at least, were approximately the same size as his own.

It was a calculated risk, but he had read his enemy well, judging that, if threatened from all sides by aggressive and vengeful *fedayner*, the Azeris would fold. They would see their impregnable fortress as a trap and consider themselves lucky if they escaped with their lives.

If they only believed half of the atrocity stories circulating after the loss of their Khodjali firebase, the Azeri garrison would expect Karabagh troops, who had spent the winter digging the bodies of family and friends out of the frozen ruins of their homes in Stepanakert, to play rough.

At the southern end of the battlefield, Ashot *Oskolka* Ghulian's men, marching over the mountains from Avetaranots, drove the Azeris from their positions on the Kirs peaks which dominated the country between Shoushi and Lachin. *Oskolka* means fragmentation in Russian; they called Ghulyan that, with black humor, because his body was full of pieces of grenade from earlier battles. In Eastern Armenian, they called him Ashot *Bekor*, which means the same thing.

The Armenians described him as a "holy fool", seeing in him an inspired, crazy, courage that brought victory when victory seemed inconceivable.

Having secured the two peaks, Ghulian and his 1ˢᵗ Company moved up to join in the attack on the walls of Shoushi.

The *fedayner* opened the battle at 2:30 am with an artillery and rocket barrage.

Ago Karapetian's men, with white crosses painted on the backs of their field jackets and on their equipment, for both sides wore the same ex-Soviet *afghanka* uniforms, forded the Karintak stream and stormed the northeast wall of the fortress.

On their right, Valeri Chitchyan's infantry advanced in two columns parallel to the main road from Stepanakert to Shoushi. With them was their only armor, the T-72[74] tank commanded by Gagic Avsharian. Beside the number '442', it was also decorated with white crosses which distinguished it from an almost identical Azeri T-72 coming down the road toward it from Shoushi.[75]

The commander of the Azeri tank advancing against the approaching Karabagh troops was, in fact, a Baku Jew named Albert Agarunov.

The two tanks fired simultaneously at a range of 400 yards.

Avsharian was a former Soviet tank officer but he had served in a unit equipped with T-64s.[76] He had been obliged to ask Ohanian, whose command had included a T-72 company, for a quick conversion course before he could take No.442 into battle.

Agarunov scored the first hit with his 125mm smoothbore[77] just as Avsharian opened his hatch to get a better view of what was happening up the road. Although badly burned, Avsharian was thrown clear, then pulled to safety by men of Ruslan Israelian's Reconnaissance Company. No.442's driver, Ashot, and gunner, Shahen, were both killed.

Agarunov, their adversary, survived this battle but was killed a few days later in the fighting at Verin Zarislu on the Lachin road. They buried him in Baku's Avenue of the Martyrs.

At one point, the defenders of Shoushi thought they might have repulsed the Karabagh assault, although ferocious fighting continued all day around the television tower on the northern perimeter and in the prison built against the northeast wall.

Then men of Gagic Sargsyan's 4th Company broke through the Azeri defenses in the northern sector.

Defenders started to slip away. 'Cossack', a Russian *kontraktnik* officer on the Azeri payroll, used the radio to order his men to pull out, leaving Orujev, nominal commander of the garrison, with little choice but to follow.

Sporadic fighting continued through the night. At dawn, Karabagh infantry moved through the silent town, suspecting an ambush, but the defenders had gone. One of the last to leave was Shamil Basayev, the Chechen, who later built a considerable reputation as a guerrilla leader in his own country.

Before mid-day, the Armenian tricolour[78] was flying over the Ghazanchetsots Cathedral, which the shrewd Azeris had been using as their main ammunition depot, sure that it was safe from Armenian gunners.

It was time to draw breath, and take stock. The Karabagh 1st, 4th, 6th, Akhnakhbur and Baluja Companies and the Reconnaissance Company, particularly distinguished themselves in the fighting for Shoushi. The *Dashnak* battalion had swept the mountain and moorland south of Shoushi clear of Azeri troops and now blocked the Lachin road.

Ter-Tatevosian reported that sixty of his men were killed and 250 wounded, and that Azeri and *kontraktnik* killed in action totalled about 200, with an estimated 600-700 wounded.

Orujev estimated that Karabagh losses were higher, and reported that his Azeri forces lost 159 killed and twenty-two missing in action.

◆        ◆        ◆

Retreating Azeri troops rallied and on 12 May launched a desperate counter-attack with their remaining armor at Verin Zarislu on the road south from Shoushi. After four or five hours of heavy fighting, *Dashnak* infantry, commanded by Albert Alaverdian, forced them back. Fighting continued on and around the Lachin road for several days, but the Azeris proved unable to mount any other serious counter-attack.

Azeri air attacks intensified in other areas in response to the Karabagh victory. Avdour, Mjurishen and Norshen in the Martuni region were attacked, as were Shosh and Krasni. Azeri armored forces started to build up pressure on the eastern and northeastern approaches to Stepanakert, but an Azeri attack on Togh, northwest of Ghadrut, was beaten back.

Aghdam, with its huge stockpile of munitions, was now the main firebase from which the bombardment of Stepanakert continued, as the capital was within range of batteries in the Aghdam area. The Azeris, who had inherited a share of the Soviet Caspian Flotilla, brought up 100mm naval guns to the Aghdam railhead, to supplement their *Grad* missile and tube artillery batteries.

After clearing the road south of Shoushi and driving the Azeris from a dozen firebases and villages that OMON troops had "cleansed" of Armenians a year earlier in the course of Azerification, Karabagh troops captured Lachin and Akhavno on 18 May and reached the frontier of the Republic of Armenia. The Lachin Corridor, lifeline between Karabagh and the rest of the world, was open.

Engineers, aided by battalions of volunteers, threw themselves into the work of rebuilding the badly-neglected road so that supply convoys could reach Stepanakert, and hospital dispensaries and food stores could be restocked.

The Baku government's inability to defend Khodjali brought down Mutalibov's pro-Moscow regime on 6 March 1992, and it was Yaqub K. Mamedov's interim government that was in power when Shoushi fell on 9 May.

After this new disaster, Mutalibov, blaming both Khodjali and Shoushi on his political enemies in Baku, was able to regain some appearance of power from 14-18 May, when he was again ousted.

# THE AZERIS STRIKE BACK (JUNE TO DECEMBER 1992)

A new interim government took over in Baku as Karabagh and Armenian troops forced open the Lachin Corridor and restored land communications between Nagorno-Karabagh and the rest of the world. It was headed by *Musavat* leader Isa Y. Gambar and consequently had a pro-Turkish complexion. Gambar immediately opened talks with officials in the Turkish defense ministry. It didn't look as if the Azeris were going to be able to solve their Karabagh problem without some outside help.

Elections were held in Azerbaijan on 7 June and pro-Turkish Azerbaijan Popular Front leader Abulfaz Elchibey won decisively, proposing to distance Azerbaijan from the CIS, and, most emphatically, to solve the problem of the *Karabaghtsi*.

"If there is a single Armenian left in Karabagh this October, Azeris will hang him in Baku's Central Square," was his boast, and within a week of being sworn in as president, Elchibey launched an invigorated army against Nagorno-Karabagh's northern frontier, while increasing pressure on the eastern and southeastern fronts.

Several thousand infantry and an estimated 150 tanks and armored fighting vehicles, artillery and *Grad* missile batteries, as well as a squadron of the Sukhoi Su-25 ground-attack aircraft that NATO calls *Frogfoot*, were involved in the Azeri *blitzkrieg*.

The Karabagh forces fell apart. Within days, Shahumian, northern Mardakert, and eastern Askeran regions were overrun and 40,000 people were driven from their looted and burning villages.

In fact, by the end of September, the advancing Azeri forces had restored Baku's authority over 48 per cent of the territory of the Nagorno-Karabagh Republic.

The Azeris were ten miles from Stepanakert, which was being pounded by the Su-25s with both smart and dumb bombs. At one end of the spectrum were the 500kg laser-guided bombs[79]; at the other, cluster bombs delivered in packages, with the effect of a massive shotgun blast. The anti-personnel cluster bombs were used specifically to encourage the refugees on their way and to break the nerve of the rest of the population.

All along the front, towns and villages from Vank to Martuni came under air, artillery and missile attack. Elchibey was well on the way to making good on his threat.

A number of factors contributed to this abrupt reversal of fortune.

On the Karabagh side, many of the Armenian *fedayner* who had fought valiantly at Shoushi had gone home to the Republic of Armenia, where work and family responsibilities called. By the end of May it had looked as if the war was all but over.

This optimism also affected the *Karabaghtsi*. They did not expect the Azeris to make so rapid a recovery, although their losses of men and matériel at Shoushi and on the Lachin road had not been heavy. They expected the main Azeri counter-attack, when one came, to come from the east with an attempt to recapture Shoushi and to close the road to Armenia.

But the routes up to Stepanakert from the east wind through mountain country, not at all suitable for the effective deployment of the Azeri main battle tanks. Attacks they did make from this direction did not fare well. Ghadrut, which commanded the main road from the southeast was surrounded on 15 August, but the *fedayner* fought off the Azeri attackers. The little mountain town never fell.

A year later, to the day, the Azeris came back to Ghadrut in force, to avenge their 1992 humiliation. Once again their attack failed; the Artsakh flag continued to wave over Ghadrut.

◆     ◆     ◆

And on the Azeri side, Elchibey was able to recruit forty NATO-trained Turkish army officers, seconded regulars or recently-retired, to help plan his campaign and lick his troops into shape.

He was also able to rally a number of paramilitary formations, such as Iskander Hamidov's ultra-nationalist Gray Wolves, who had loathed Mutalibov but who now threw themselves wholeheartedly into the fight.

The commander of one such unit, Col. Surat Husseinov, had done some deals with his Ukrainian friend, Maj.Gen. Valery Vitalievich Shcherbak, commander of the 104th Guards Airborne Division, and with the officers of the 31st Guards Motor Rifle Diivision, both based at Gandža, that resulted in the transfer to Husseinov's 709th Azeri Brigade of far more than its share of the Soviet 4th Army matériel allocated to Azerbaijan by the CIS's 15 May 1992 Tashkent Treaty on Collective Security.[80]

Not only did Husseinov, a wealthy black-marketeer in private life, although little over thirty, inherit a strong force of T-72 tanks and other armored vehicles, he inherited their crews. Yeltsin's Russia had too little money to pay its soldiers; oil-rich Azerbaijan looked like a much more promising paymaster. In the short term, Husseinov had roubles and vodka to motivate a powerful fighting force.

The APF defense minister, Rahim Gaziev, was another who sought to maintain good relations with Moscow, although his cabinet colleagues were demonstrably pro-Turkish.

This accumulation of weapons, and *kontraktniki* to use them effectively, was a major factor contributing to the success of the Azeri offensive in June 1992.

◆    ◆    ◆

With Azeri columns pouring into the heart of Karabagh, the Armenian government was not slow to ask Moscow to level the playing field. They found sympathetic ears in the Kremlin. Boris Yeltsin got on well with Ter-Petrosian and was, in any case, concerned to maintain a military balance in the strategically sensitive Caucasus. The Cold War might be over but Turkey had not gone away, and had one of the few really dangerous armies close to the Russian frontier.

◆    ◆    ◆

The inhabitants of the northern region of Shahumian, who had been evicted from their homes by the Azeris during *Operation Koltso* in the spring of 1991, knew what was coming in June 1992. Almost the entire population, together with the people of the Mardakert region and other areas in the path of the Azeri tanks, dropped whatever they were doing and fled south, toward Stepanakert.

Azeri forces also thrust into the Mardakert region from the west, down the Tartar gorge, seizing and burning the large village of Haterk, west of the Sarsang Reservoir.

On 4 July, the town of Mardakert was attacked from three directions in a classic combined arms offensive orchestrated by Turkish staff officers.[81] Thousands of Azeri infantry supported by seventy tanks and armored fighting vehicles, and by tube and missile artillery, as well as by Sukhoi Su-25 *Frogfoot* ground-attack aircraft from Sital-Chaj air base, forced the Karabagh defenders to withdraw precipitately.

Azeri troops entering Mardakert noted with joyful surprise that the inhabitants had taken few of their possessions, so sudden had been their departure.

Although many of the refugees left their furniture and appliances behind, the only road up which Karabagh reinforcements could be brought into action was clogged with an avalanche of terrified people.

Only a miracle could save the Armenians of Nagorno-Karabagh.

◆    ◆    ◆

In Yerevan and Gyumri, Armenian officials talked to commanders of ex-Soviet 7th Army and air force units, and received a sympathetic hearing.

In short order, a squadron of Mil Mi-24 gunships, which the Russians call *Krokodil* and NATO call *Hind*, took off from Gyumri on a southeast heading.

What resulted was a major reappraisal of the situation by the Russian *kontraktnik* tankers on the ground. Chasing the refugees and a handful of *fedayner* armed with shotguns and the odd AK-47 had been an amusing turkey-shoot, but slugging it out with their own Frontal Aviation gunships was something entirely different.

The Azeri command had to decide quickly whether they were in an undeclared war with the Russian Federation which retained ownership of the Mi-24s, or whether the Gyumri gunships were piloted by freelance Russians, hired for roubles and vodka on the same basis as their own T-72 tank crews.

While they were deciding, the *Karabaghtsi* got enough volunteers into the line to hold the Azeri advance along the Drmbon-Gyoulatagh axis.

The *fedayner* were soon forced back into the hills that separate the valleys of the Tartar and Khachenaget rivers, and into the foothills north of Askeran, but the momentum of the Azeri advance had been broken for the moment.

The western end of this new defensive line was anchored by the monastery of Gandzasar—the Monte Cassino of Nagorno-Karabagh. It stood on a hilltop with views eastward down the Khachenaget valley and west to the blue mountain ranges of Karvachar.

The Azeri army was advancing across the ridge to the north.

If Gandzasar fell, the Azeris could outflank the last strong defensive position north of Stepanakert and roll up the *fedayner* line from west to east.

Gandzasar means *treasure mountain*, for silver was once mined there. The monastery and its ancient church, standing in surroundings of incredible beauty, have an air of holiness apparent to even the least religious of visitors.

Seeing no incongruity in blasting walls built in 1216, with Space Age missiles and cluster bombs, the Azeris threw everything they had at Gandzasar to break the resistance of its defenders.

Ter Hovhannes, warrior-priest of the monastery church of St. John the Baptist, put aside his censer and took up an AK-47 to fight with the *fedayner*. With prayers and steel-cored bullets, he and his fellow *Karabaghtsi* fought off the Azeri attackers. They claimed thirty-three of the attacking planes and gunships shot down with their *Igla*[82] anti-aircraft missiles, making this the most decisive defeat suffered by the Azeri air force during the war.

The valley below is still littered with the wreckage of Azeri armor.

Unlike Monte Cassino, Gandzasar did not fall. Although pilgrims can still dig fragments of missile casing from the monastery walls, the splendid church, described as the most culturally important building in Karabagh, was miraculously undamaged.

In Stepanakert, Robert Kocharian, who had fought with the blockading force south of Shoushi in May, persuaded deputies to the council of ministers to impose martial law on 18 June under a state defense committee, of which he was to be chairman. Two days later, ministers ordered something close to a *levée en masse* to provide the personnel needed to defend the young republic, although most of those who could fight were already at the front.

All ex-Soviet reservists up to the age of forty, and officers up to fifty years of age were called up, as were women under thirty who had needed skills, such as doctors and nurses.

But the Karabagh troops were still under considerable pressure and again called for help from Armenia.

Armenian Defense Minister Vazgen Sarkisian broadcast radio appeals in Armenian and Russian for Armenian officers who had served in the Soviet forces to come and help defend Artsakh.

One of those who heard was an ailing 72-year-old in St. Petersburg.

Kristofor Ivanovich Ivanian originally came from Tblisi. Although the capital of Georgia, it had the largest Armenian population in the Transcaucasus when Ivanian was born there in 1920. His family had been Tsarist generals, and his wife was Russian; his children thoroughly Russianized. He himself was only remotely Armenian. But he was still very much a soldier.[83]

He had left the military academy for the battlefields of the Great Patriotic War. In April 1945, already a Hero of the Soviet Union, he was one of Zhukov's artillery commanders, pounding Berlin to rubble.

"I should go," he said, when he heard Sarkisian's broadcast.

"Don't be silly," said the Russian wife. "You can't stand up for more than half-an-hour at a time." Her husband was dying of cancer.

"I'm going to buy some cigarettes," said Ivanian. He didn't return.

Next day he was in Yerevan, trying to sign up. Busy volunteers, scrounging weapons and supplies and figuring out imaginative ways of getting them into the hands of the fighters in Karabagh, shunted the old Soviet *butinski* aside until the day was far gone.

Finally he snapped. "Tell your boss that Kristofor Ivanian is here to volunteer for Artsakh," he snarled.

"Are you the *K. Ivanian* who wrote all the artillery textbooks we used at the Frunze Academy?" asked an officer who overheard.

Within a couple of hours, Lt.Gen. Ivanian was talking to President Levon Ter-Petrosian, who immediately appointed him special advisor. They gave him a plush office in Yerevan, an *aide de camp,* and a secretary.

But the general hadn't come to polish an office chair. He disappeared again.

Now the Azeris were launching an attack on the southeastern front, driving headlong toward the heart of Nagorno-Karabagh. Ivanian showed up on the Fizuli road as retreating Karabagh artillerymen were trying to save their only guns from encirclement.

The general ordered them to halt and turn around. But they already had orders to fall back and save the guns. An argument took place there on the bullet-swept highway. Generals who once pounded the Third Reich into oblivion do not lose arguments, so the battery turned and fought, Ivanian laying the guns. The Azeris were stopped dead by well-directed artillery fire and lost some of their own guns and a *Grad* missile battery.

Given a breathing space, the Nagorno-Karabagh command co-opted the general and assigned him to develop a training program for junior officers. As the army was fighting on four fronts, the students spent more time in combat than in their classrooms in what had once been the Azeri firebase of Khodjali, but was soon called Ivanovka, in the general's honor.

Ivanian's next assignment would be to the northern front, to the mountains and forests of Shahumian and Mardakert. Although he was given a *dacha* in Stepanakert for his wife, and was suffering from medical problems that would have killed a weaker man, the general continued to live in the field with his troops, touring their mountain positions on horseback[84] almost daily. They hated his Stalinist approach to discipline, but at the same time loved and revered him.

While the civilian population of the Shahumian region had fled when the Azeri tanks roared over the horizon in June, many of the *fedayner* had not. Led by Shahen Meghrian[85], these guerrillas retreated into the canyons and forests of the Mrav Mountains, to pose an ongoing threat to the Azeri lines of communication.

Military convoys and the hordes of civilian looters from Gandža and Jevlach, who followed the Azeri army, were all fair game. For a year the *fedayner* operated far behind the Azeri lines, supplied occasionally by helicopter, but living off the country and, for the most part, fighting with arms and ammunition captured from the enemy.

At one point, the Azeris had as many as 5,000 men hunting fifty *Yegh-nigner*, as the partisans called themselves. As the brutal Mrav winter closed in, conditions became dire for the guerrillas, hunted from the air by Azeri gunships and tracked on the ground by OMON bloodhounds.

Meghrian was wounded in one battle, then, with a dozen other casualties, was killed when their Mi-8 medevac helicopter was brought down by an Azeri missile.

Vahe Baghdassarian, who had left his medical studies in Yerevan a few months short of graduation to serve with the *Dashnak* battalion at Shoushi and Lisagor, took command. The *Yeghnigner*, hard hit by their losses, attacked the Azeris with renewed ferocity, achieving results out of all proportion to their numbers and paving the way for the eventual liberation of much of the northern region.

Baghdassarian, leading from the front as always, was killed in 1993 attacking an Azeri machine gun position.

Most of the non-*Karabaghtsi* who fought for the Nagorno-Karabagh Republic were from the Republic of Armenia, but there were some volunteers from the *Diaspora*. The most colorful was Monte Melkonian, otherwise known as Avo.

Avo was born in northern California on 25 November 1957, and was by profession an archeologist; by vocation a freedom fighter. He had been leader of one of the factions of ASALA the Armenian Secret Army for the Liberation of Armenia, whose business was assassinating Turkish diplomats. He had been on the run for years.

Before joining ASALA in the spring of 1980, he had fought in the Lebanese Civil War[86] in an Armenian militia allied with the Palestine Liberation Organization and opposed to the Christian Phalange.

He was a Berkeley-educated Marxist but driven by fanatical devotion to the Armenian cause. "If we lose Artsakh, we close the book on the history of our people," said Monte Melkonian.

And he was a man of rare integrity. He was given command of the exposed Martuni region of eastern Karabagh, and surprised his irregular troops with his puritanical approach to bribery, to looting, and, strangest of all to post-Soviet soldiers, to vodka. He forbade his men to drink alcohol or to mistreat prisoners.

He was killed by an Azeri sniper near Marzili, southeast of Aghdam, on 12 June 1993.

◆    ◆    ◆

Once the intervention of the 7th Army gunships broke the momentum of the Azeri armored columns, their advance started to bog down. Their air cover had also taken a beating.

*Kontraktnik* technical and tactical expertise could not turn the various disparate elements that Elchibey had mobilized into an army capable of fighting a sustained campaign against a foe that was fighting for survival and was getting very good at fighting..

And the Azeri main force was now entering mountainous country in the heart of Nagorno-Karabagh. This terrain posed more complex tactical problems for tank commanders than the open steppe of the northeast.

Every day that passed took the Azeris a day further from victory, and bought the Nagorno-Karabagh troops time to solve their own problems.

In some ways they faced the same difficulties as the Azeris. The *fedayner* were united only by a common cause. On occasion, so it was reported, whole companies would take off for Yerevan to bury one of their slain comrades at Tsitsernakaberd, leaving the war to take care of itself for a day or two.

Robert Kocharian's task, as he chaired the state defense committee, was to bring order out of this chaos. In September, the regular army of the Nagorno-Karabagh Republic was formed from various *fedayn* units, and the republic was divided into six defensive regions.

One of the advantages that Nagorno-Karabagh had was that it was fighting on what soldiers call "interior lines", which is to say that troops could be moved from one front to another relatively easily. Later in the month, for example, the Central Defensive Region's 2nd and 3rd Battalions were sent up to Arajadzor and Vaghouhas, to help stabilize the northern front.

The flip side of the coin was that Karabagh was under attack from all directions.

The Azeris did not have the advantage of interior lines. While able to keep the pressure on the Nagorno-Karabagh Republic from various points, they could not, to take one example, easily move troops from the Kashounik pocket up to the Mardakert front. Nor, if they achieved a breakthrough, could they easily switch troops from other fronts to exploit the success.

During September and October 1992, the Azeri forces maintained pressure from the Martuni Steppe, on the eastern front.

The Lachin Corridor also came under heavy attack, with bombardment from Topaguch Mountain near Khtsaberd.

Then, on 12 October Karabagh forces captured Topaguch.

Two days later, the Azeris attacked from Gochaz Mountain, north of the Lachin Corridor, but were driven back, losing their foothold in the Saribaba area.

As both sides hunkered down for another hard winter, neither side had a clear advantage. The Nagorno-Karabagh Republic still included the airstrip at Ivanovka. Shoushi was still secure, and the Lachin Corridor from Armenia was still open, but the Azeris and their allies, who had joined battle in the second half of 1992 were very different soldiers from those who had lost Shoushi in the Spring.

The Karabagh troops had also matured as a result of some brutally hard lessons. If they had survived, it was because they had been very lucky. They could not count on such luck again; it was clear that the 7$^{th}$ Army gunships would not be on call. From now on, the Nagorno-Karabagh Republic would have to build a disciplined, professional self-defense force. In their favor they had a cadre of experienced ex-Soviet officers, and a corps of battle-hardened *azatamartics*, who would learn the whole art of war, if they survived long enough.

The Azeri blockade ensured that the winter of 1992-3 was terribly hard for Armenia and for Nagorno-Karabagh, but Azerbaijan had also paid a heavy price. An estimated 5,000 Azeri soldiers had been killed and 18,000 wounded up to this point in the war. Even more telling were reports that 20,000 Azeris had deserted rather than continue to fight an unwinnable war against an increasingly dangerous enemy.

Thousands of refugees on both sides had a particularly hard time during the winter months.

# KARVACHAR, AND CRISIS IN BAKU (JANUARY TO DECEMBER 1993)

Azeri forces resumed the bombardment of Artsakh towns and villages at the start of 1993, and attacked the Sardarashen-Mekhtishen area with air and armored forces.

Fighting continued on the front line near Chldran and Shravend, and in the Lachin Corridor.

Driving north across the mountains, Karabagh troops took Kichan, then Chldran, and cut the strategic Karvachar-to-Mardakert road at Drmbon. Troops from the 3$^{rd}$ and 4$^{th}$ Defensive Regions, with elements of the Central Defensive Region's 54$^{th}$ Independent Motor Rifle Battalion, broke Azeri resistance and pursued their demoralized enemy.

Although many of the surrounding villages were under Karabagh control by the end of February, the Azeris put up a stubborn fight for the Sarsang hydro-electric station and dam, but were forced eventually to abandon their positions.

In early March, Karabagh forces took Mets Shen, Maghavuz and other villages west of Mardakert.

The Azeri command ordered its western forces in Karvachar to attack Karabagh forces in the Mardakert region to relieve pressure on the communications hub of Mardakert, but the *Karabaghtsi* saw the danger and moved up the Tartar gorge to block the Azeri advance, and on 31 March captured the cathedral and monastery complex of Dadivank.

Since at least the 9$^{th}$ century, and possibly since the 4$^{th}$, Armenian pilgrims have worshiped there at the church of martyred Surp Dadi, known in the West as St. Jude Thaddeus[87], patron of hopeless causes and therefore particularly dear to the embattled *Karabaghtsi*. But Stalin, the lapsed seminarian, drew the border of the Nagorno-Karabagh *oblast* to exclude Dadivank from Christian territory, and place it inside the borders of the Karvachar region.

The Azerbaijan Soviet Socialist Republic's *oblast* of Nagorno-Karabagh, though populated largely by Christian Armenians, had been separated from the Armenian Soviet Socialist Republic by this sparsely inhabited area of mountain and moorland, whose only important town is also called Karvachar.

This piece of Azerbaijan hammered like a wedge between the two Armenian lands was an irritation to the *Karabaghtsi*. Worse, Karvachar was the open backdoor to Nagorno-Karabagh.

As early as July 1992, Azeri forces had crossed the Mrav Mountains, turned east, and thrust down the Tartar gorge into Karabagh, capturing and burning Haterk, a large Armenian village west of the Sarsang Reservoir, and threatening the rear of the *Karabaghtsi* defenders of Mardakert.

The Tartar gorge is narrow and deep and could be held by a few score men against an army, but for one thing, the helicopter. Defenders of such a feature can easily be outflanked and themselves surrounded by an enemy that has the capability to airlift commandos to their rear. This ever-present threat is why the Nagorno-Karabagh Republic command decided in March 1993 that they had to clear the Azeris out of Karvachar.

They launched their offensive on 27 March, 1993.

Over the previous three months, the reorganization of the NKR military had started to pay off. Karabagh troops had made gains near Uryan peak and Tchartar, near Martuni in the east. In early February the 54th Battalion and volunteers from the Republic of Armenia attacked Azeri positions on a broad front extending from Vaghouhas, near the bottom of the Tartar gorge, to Mardakert, and raided as far north as Haterk, Zaglic and Talysh.

Meanwhile, new tears appeared in the fabric of the Azeri war effort.

An Azeri battalion was trapped at Haterk by the advancing NKR troops, and defense minister Rahim Gaziev and Surat Husseinov, the military commander of the region, rather than mount an operation to extract it, decided that the troops were expendable.

Their decision came to the attention of interior minister Iskander Hamidov, the pro-Turkish Gray Wolf, always suspicious of the Russophiles Gaziev and Husseinov. He raised the issue in the council of ministers and forced Gaziev to try to rescue the unit, and so the unit was pulled out, but only with heavy losses.

Insulted by Hamidov's interference with his command decision, Husseinov withdrew two Azeri brigades from the front. Elchibey fired him from his post as "plenipotentiary presidential representative' and ordered him back to Baku. Husseinov declined to obey but remained in Gandža, with his private army, the 709th Brigade, in close contact with the friendly Russian 104th Guards Airborne Division.

Elchibey also fired Gaziev, who was not working out as a team player in the Baku cabinet. He had only lasted as long as he did because, like Husseinov, he was one of the few current Azeri leaders able to do business with the Russians.

❖    ❖    ❖

So when a combined NKR and Armenian force[88], commanded by a French national codenamed 'Marcel', drove across the Zod Pass from the Republic of Armenia, into the Karvachar region, and other NKR troops thrust up the Tartar gorge from Dadivank, the Azeris put up only a feeble resistance. By 2 April, Karvachar, the regional capital, had fallen to the Armenian-NKR forces.[89] Most of the town's defenders had tossed away their weapons, stripped off their uniforms, and mixed with the fleeing civil population. But flight wasn't easy.

Thomas Goltz, an American journalist, witnessed the collapse of the Azeri resistance, and the valiant efforts made by Azeri and *kontraktnik* aircrew to rescue civilian refugees from Karvachar, scraping over the 12,000-foot Mrav Mountains with loads of seventy-five passengers in Mil Mi-8 helicopters rated for twenty-four.[90]

Having an Azeri wife and a great sympathy for the Azeri people, Goltz was enraged to discover after the debacle, that it had taken Surat Husseinov's 709th Brigade tanks and *Grad* missile batteries two weeks to travel the 50 miles from their base in Gandža to the foothills of the Mrav. They never went into action at all, as NKR troops seized the Omar Pass on 5 April and completed mopping-up operations in Karvachar ten days later.

His enemies claimed that, at this stage in his career, Husseinov, a hero of the 1992 campaign, was more interested in keeping his forces intact and playing politics inside Azerbaijan, than in fighting the Armenians.

Complaints about Russian involvement in the war, led to pressure for the withdrawal of the last of the 62,000 Russian soldiers who had been stationed in Azerbaijan. This was accomplished a year ahead of schedule on 28 May 1993 when the 6,500 men of the 104th Guards Airborne Division pulled out of Gandža, making Azerbaijan the only ex-Soviet republic with no major Russian unit on its territory.[91]

As Husseinov had maintained close relations with the 104th which had an allocation of 348 BMDs (airborne infantry fighting vehicles) and 31 ASU-85s (85mm self-propelled airborne assault guns), its departure meant another windfall of matériel for his forces.

Only a detachment of Russian technicians and guards remained at the early-warning station at Gabala[92], and a limited number of frontier troops supported Azerbaijan's border guards on the Araks River.

◆     ◆     ◆

In June, Elchibey sent troops to Gandža to disarm Husseinov, who now posed a serious threat to the Baku regime. After some skirmishing in and around Gandža between Husseinov's men and the troops from Baku, Husseinov shook off Elchibey's men and marched on the capital.

At this point, Elchibey fled Baku and went home to his native village, Keleki, in Nakhichevan. Coincidentally, another Nakhichevan native[93], who had been biding his time in Moscow and possibly talking to old friends in the Kremlin[94], returned to Baku.

So it was that when Husseinov entered the capital, he found that Heidar Aliev, Azerbaijan's former Communist Party and KGB boss, had already been elected speaker of the Azeri parliament.

Negotiations between Aliev and Husseinov left Aliev free to run for president in October 1993, and Husseinov for the office of prime minister, with additional responsibility for the key ministries of defense, internal affairs and national security.

Meanwhile, Col. Alakram Alekper Gumbatov, who had earlier raised a brigade to fight in Karabagh, proclaimed an independent Talish-Mugan Republic in southern Azerbaijan, with Lenkoran as its capital.

The pro-Russian ex-minister, Rahim Gaziev was somehow involved, and Goltz suggests that the objective of both the Husseinov and Gumbatov coups may have been to bring Mutalibov back from Moscow and return him to power.[95]

Goltz also saw Russia's hand at work in the events surrounding Elchibey's departure. Elchibey, suffering from "depression", induced perhaps by the fear that the Russians were on his case in earnest, was gone. Keleki was as far as he could get from Baku without leaving Azeri territory. He did not formally renounce the presidency.

Aliev took care of that for him on 29 August 1993, with a vote of confidence on Elchibey's performance. The deputies sitting in the *Milli Mejlis*[96] under Aliev's cold eye, did not, it seemed, have any confidence at all in the absent Elchibey.

An election, of sorts, was called on 3 October 1993. Heidar Aliev won the presidency with 98.8 per cent of the vote, against two other candidates.

Certainly Elchibey's APF-*Musavat* government had been anti-Russian from the outset. It had even refused to stay in the CIS, a decision that Aliev reversed in September 1993 to Moscow's relief. The Russians had been understandably nervous about having a possibly hostile regime on their borders with Turkey and Iran; nervous too about a Moslem regime close to Chechnya, where trouble was brewing.[97]

Aliev hardly needed the lesson of the Husseinov and Gumbatov coups to see the danger represented by the thirty private armies, of varying sizes, engaged in supporting or subverting the Azeri military. Most politically ambitious Azeris had seen private armies loyal to themselves rather than to the Azeri state, as being prerequisites for any pursuit of power. The equation was clear: Armed men plus tanks equal political credibility.

First, Aliev decided to deal with Gumbatov. Within a couple of months his troops had broken Gumbatov's forces and taken his capital at Lenkoran. Gumbatov was in exile over the border in Iran, but Aliev was talking extradition.

He began to pressure other military commanders to bring their forces into the Aliev fold. Some held out longer than others. Husseinov, for example, still had strong power bases in Gandža and Jevlach, and was well equipped with T-72 tanks with his name: *SURAT* painted on their turrets in big white Cyrillic letters, as well as other matériel. Neither he nor Aliev saw their June power-sharing deal as final.

◆      ◆      ◆

Meanwhile, at the front, NKR forces from Martuni and Ghadrut captured several Azeri strongpoints. The Azeris responded with a renewed offensive, but that effort ground to a halt on 12 June.

Then NKR troops feinted in various directions to disguise their real goal of recapturing the important town of Mardakert, which they did at the end of June.

The Azeris retaliated by intensifying the bombardment of Karabagh towns and villages from their firebase at Aghdam, and from other sites supplied with missiles and shells from the Aghdam railhead. It seemed likely that the *Karabaghtsi* would soon have to move against Aghdam, but Surat Husseinov declared that he would personally lead his troops to save the town from Mardakert's fate.

Giving the matter more thought, Husseinov remembered that Aghdam had always been a stronghold of Elchibey's APF. Elchibey was history, but not wanting to do anything to change this, Husseinov decided it might be expedient to let events take their course in Aghdam. He went back on his promise of aid.

NKR troops moved north and south of the town in mid-July and on 23-24 closed in. In accordance with their usual practice, they left an escape route open for Aghdam's 160,000 inhabitants, but captured large quantities of munitions that the Azeris did not have time to take away.

The *Karabaghtsi* then proceeded to dismantle the town to provide building materials for the reconstruction of shattered Stepanakert and other Karabagh towns that had been levelled by the guns and missile batteries of Aghdam. Only the Aghdam mosque, with its twin minarets, and the cemetery were left intact.

In the late summer of 1993, to lessen his dependence on militias raised by potential rivals for power, Aliev sent his foreign minister, Rovshan Jivadov, to Kabul. His task there was to negotiate with Prime Minister Gulbuddin Hekmatyar[98] for the services of between 1,500 and 2,500 of his Hizb-i Wahdat *mujahidin.* [99] At least an American recruiter who was involved in the deal, said they were Hizb-i Wahdat *mujahidin,* although others described them as "clueless refugee kids rounded up on the streets of Peshawar".[100]

By 1988 the Hizb-i Wahdat (Unity Party) had consolidated, under Iranian sponsorship, most of Afghanistan's Shiite *mujahidin.* Almost all of the Shiites were ethnic Hazaras from central Afghanistan, traditionally at odds with the dominant Pashtuns, who are Sunni Moslems. Their leader, Hekmatyar, who also had an important power-base in Paktia[101], was prime minister from March 1993 to January 1994. As he was heavily involved in the civil war that ended with the Taliban's 1996 take-over, it seems unlikely that he would send his best troops to Baku.

But Afghan troops did go to Azerbaijan. Their commanders were American[102] or Turkish, and their headquarters was at Bash Karvend, northeast of Aghdam, until NKR troops took the town in April 1994 and drove them out.

Significant numbers of Russian or Ukrainian *kontraktniki* already provided most of the leadership and technical expertise for Azeri artillery and armored formations, and most aircrew were, of course, *kontraktniki.*

Aliev's elimination of the private armies was undertaken for internal political reasons and left a void at the front, despite the recruitment of mercenaries. The Azeri forces had to rely more and more on conscripts and on young men who were, frankly, press-ganged on city streets to provide the numbers required.

Kurdish youths, outside the mainstream of Azeri political life, were particularly targeted in this hunt for cannon-fodder. The Lezgin and Talish minorities, both suspected of secessionist tendencies, were also disproportionately represented in Aliev's human waves, if the evidence of identity documents discovered on the bodies of the dead can be believed.

These reluctant soldiers were often only half-trained, for human waves do not need training, just professional encouragement to keep rolling forward. NKR troops say they saw the unsympathetic *mujahidin* driving these reluctant mobs forward onto the NKR guns.

Relations between the Afghans and the Azeri people were further strained as a result of the Afghan perception that the Azeris were totally lacking in Shiite fervor. Three generations of Soviet rule had left a secular population that hardly understood the concept of *jihad.*

Whatever the truth of the matter, the *mujahidin* came to be perceived as the backbone of the Azeri infantry, as the NKR troops sought to clear the Azeris out of the Kashounik-Dzhebrail-Kovsakan pocket between Nagorno-Karabagh and the Iranian border. If they could achieve this, the Karabagh forces would considerably shorten the front they had to defend, and reduce an ongoing threat to the vital Lachin Corridor.

It was a Hizb-i Wahdat *mujahidin* battalion that spearheaded a surprise Azeri attack near Dzhebrail on 21 October.[103] Two days later, counter-attacking NKR troops captured documents in Pashto and Dari[104], photographs of Afghan fighters at various tourist sites in Azerbaijan, and lists of military terms translated from Azeri into Dari.

The balance of 1993 was taken up with see-sawing battles on the eastern and southeastern fronts. NKR troops thrust across the Mil Steppe as far as Bejlagan, 25 miles east of Fizuli, but made no attempt to hold the position. The raid was intended rather as a demonstration that the *Karabaghtsi* could go anywhere they wanted and, in this instance, threaten Azerbaijan's railroad system.

The NKR troops also fought their way down the Araks River, which separated Azerbaijan from Iran, as far as Goradiz, having cleared most of the Kashounik-Dzhebrail-Kovsakan pocket.

Then in mid-December, Aliev launched another large-scale, human-wave offensive, forcing NKR troops to withdraw from Talysh and Maghavuz in the northern Mardakert region. Azeri armor put heavy pressure on NKR positions on the eastern front north of Aghdam and, further south, *mujahidin* played a key role in recapturing Goradiz on 6 January 1994.

# SECOND KARVACHAR CAMPAIGN (JANUARY TO MAY 1994)

The Azeri offensive on the eastern front was still going well when Aliev ordered his troops across the Omar Pass into Karvachar on New Year's Eve, 1993.

That is as much as has been told to the grieving people of Azerbaijan, a few of whom still hope that lost loved ones might return from some Armenian *gulag.*

The NKR command, under heavy pressure in the east and fearful that the Azeri tanks would break through to Aghdam or even Stepanakert, pulled back the raw troops of the Armenian Vanadzor Division to the town of Karvachar, obliging the Azeris to stretch their line of communication which ran along the old logging road through the Omar Pass.

As the Azeris approached the regional capital, they took a calculated risk in leaving the Zod Pass, which crossed the mountains from Armenia, in their rear. The road across the pass was no more than a rough track and frequently impassable in winter, but it had been used to good effect by Armenian troops during the previous year.

However, it was from Karabagh that battle-hardened battalions moved up at the end of January 1994 to attack the Azeri lines of communication. From the outset, they posed a serious threat, but what really defeated the Azeris was the winter weather.

Snow might have been expected on the 12,000-foot mountains, but the snow that started to fall on 12 February was heavy, even by the standards of the Mrav.

Azeri supply lines were cut, but living off the country was not an option in the desolate Karvachar region. The NKR command seized its advantage and closed in for the kill.

Unlike the tough Karabagh mountaineers, the majority of the Azeri troops were press-ganged youths from the streets of Baku, Sumgait and Lenkoran, in the sub-tropical lowlands beside the Caspian. Fighting to the death in deep snow did not come easily to boys who had never even seen snow.

When it seemed that part of the army might still be able to escape, the Azeri chief of staff, Gen. Najmedtin Sadyqov, a crony of Prime Minister Surat Husseinov, ordered his men to storm the NKR blocking positions. Two Azeri brigades that attempted to fight their way out were brought to bay in the southern approaches to the Omar Pass on 18-20 February.

NKR gunners shelled the snowfields above the Azeris with *Grad* launchers they had captured at Aghdam the previous July. Hundreds of men were swept away in avalanches. Other Azeri soldiers were killed in friendly fire incidents when their own *Grad* batteries bombarded them.

Then rumors started to circulate among the Azeri troops that they had been written off and that Baku neither would nor could rescue the trapped army, or even supply it with ammunition or food. "No point in feeding dead men," they muttered bitterly to each other as they trudged through the snow.

The number of Azeri dead is still classified *secret* in Baku. Best estimates are that the Azeris lost about 4,000 men, and the NKR and Armenian allies about 2,000 in the Karvachar battles of 1994 that proved to be the bloodiest of the war.[105]

Eight decades earlier, the Turkish 9th Corps had perished in similar circumstances in the mountains at Sarikamish. Enver Pasha made the Armenians scapegoats for his defeat, and the genocide of 1915 followed. The

*Karabaghtsi* saw that their annihilation of the Azeris, little brothers of the Turks, in the Mrav battles, closed the circle with an element of poetic justice.

Over the next few weeks, the other Azeri offensives gained some ground, but then bogged down, and many of the recent gains were lost to NKR counter-attacks. An Azeri force was encircled and destroyed at Akop Kamari on the eastern front, and NKR troops defending Aghdam broke the teeth of the Azeri attack and, in the first week of May, pushed north, about two-thirds of the way to Barda.

The Azeris feared that the Karabagh objective was the key road and rail junction of Jevlach, 15 miles beyond Barda. If Jevlach fell, Azerbaijan would be effectively cut in two. Nothing the Azeri army had done recently gave Baku any reason to suppose that the NKR forces could be stopped.

But having achieved their goal of a defensible cease-fire line, the NKR did not worry too much about Jevlach, or even about leaving in Azeri hands the northern rim of Mardakert region, which was closer to Azeri bases than it was to Stepanakert, or the town of Goradiz on the Iranian frontier, which Aliev could reinforce and supply by rail. In all cases the costs of taking and holding these areas outweighed any possible benefits.

With some pressure from Russia, and a feeling on both sides that further bloodshed was unlikely to do more than achieve minor adjustments to an eventual cease-fire line, parliamentary delegations from the CIS members, and Karen Baburian, speaker of the Nagorno-Karabagh parliament, met in Bishkek, the capital of Kyrgyzstan, and drafted what became known as the Bishkek Protocol.

This blueprint for a truce was eventually signed by the concerned parties and the truce has held, more or less, until the time of writing. Both sides are dug in along a cease-fire line that separates almost all of Nagorno-Karabagh plus a defensible security zone, from Azerbaijan.

Despite the truce, shots are exchanged almost every day between NKR and Azeri soldiers somewhere along the cease-fire line; blood is shed quite often. But neither army has attacked the other since the spring of 1994.

While Christian Armenians have their Karabagh homeland and a defensible frontier, Azeri and Turkish blockades cause considerable economic problems and personal hardship in both Armenia and the Nagorno-Karabagh Republic. But they fought to survive and did survive.

They won the war. Now they saw that their task was to avoid losing the peace.

# THE AFTERMATH

Karabagh's defenses are clearly there to stay, with a 112-mile long anti-tank ditch stretching from Armenia in the north to Iran in the south. The ditch is complemented by a network of well-planned trenches, bunkers and gun positions with clear fields of fire, calculated to block any attack the Azeris could mount. Since the 1994 cease-fire, Karabagh's T-72s have been held in strategic reserve in Stepanakert.

The frontier positions are defended by well-disciplined soldiers of serious aspect who watch their Azeri neighbors day and night across a mile of no-man's-land.

Security is tight near the front line and, indeed, throughout Karabagh.

On the Azeri side there is no ditch or fortification that might suggest that the Baku government accepts the cease-fire line as permanent, or even as an acceptable medium-term solution. The Azeri positions are observation posts, or "trip-wire" intruder alarms, rather than serious defenses. The Azeris clearly do not believe that the *Karabaghtsi* will attack, and if they do, trust that they will be able to bring international pressure to bear on the Armenians long before NKR forces could reach Baku.

Or so they hope, although in the summer of 1993, both sides realized that the fighting ability of the Azeri army had eroded to such a degree that, had they wished, the *Karabaghtsi* could have reached Baku within two days.[106]

Fortunately for both sides, the NKR command realized that a battle in the streets of a city of 1.7 million, against people who were now fighting for their homes, rather than for the aggrandisement of their political class, would be suicidal.

Today's Azeri soldiers look like the same kind of reluctant conscripts who were beaten in 1993 and again in 1994. With a few exceptions, they look as if they would expect to be beaten again if hostilities were renewed. Their officers spend as much time as possible on R&R in the capital, 150 miles behind the lines. Morale, even in the military academies is, by all accounts, poor. Turkish instructors have gone home in disgust.

There is no evidence of *kontraktniki*, financed with petro-dollars, although it would not be hard for the Baku government to raise a mercenary army of Russian or Ukrainian ex-soldiers if the will and the resources were available.

American, British or Israeli private military corporations would also be willing to recruit an army, but at rather greater expense.

Already Pakistan, as a United States proxy, is providing military training and equipment, although in 2004 the Azeri parliament passed a law prohibiting the stationing of foreign troops on Azeri soil. This was seen as a move to reassure both Moscow and Tehran that rumors that American bases were to be established in Azerbaijan were unfounded..

However, Azerbaijan's skies are patrolled fraternally by F-16 C/D Vipers of 181 Pars and 182 Atmaca Interceptor Squadrons of the Turkish 2nd Tactical Air Force, based at Diyarbakir. Both the Turks and the Americans, whose flights to Afghanistan and Central Asia must pass through the Georgia-Azerbaijan corridor[107], appreciate the strategic importance of Azerbaijan's military airfields.

Azerbaijan is inescapably a pivotal power where Europe and Asia and Russia and the Middle East meet. The fact that it is floating on a sea of oil and

natural gas makes it no less interesting to the great and not-so-great powers.

If fortune smiles on oil-rich Azerbaijan, the Americans will send Special
Forces advisors to breathe life into the Azeri army as they did into Georgia's. Protection of the oil and gas pipelines against Al Quaeda, or other
unspecified terrorist threats, would provide a more marketable rationale
for military support, than laying the groundwork for the ethnic cleansing
of Nagorno-Karabagh.

Bill Richardson, energy secretary[108] in the Clinton administration, noted
in November 1998 that the United States had made "a substantial political
investment in the Caspian".

"It's important," he said, "that both the pipeline map and the politics
come out right."

United States' policy with regard to the Caspian has matured since then,
but not changed direction. There are oil industry lobbyists in Washington
who argue that giving the Azeris *carte blanche* to do what they have to do
to solve their "Armenian problem", would be a small price to pay for
maintaining good relations with a state that has as much oil as Azerbaijan.

This would mean military support for Azerbaijan, direct or indirect. Once
the Baku regime had an effective army, the cease fire could easily come to
an end. But, given Russia's interest in its "near abroad", and in Armenia in
particular, some analysts fear that a renewed war could, like events in Sara-
jevo in 1914, ignite a serious conflagration.[109]

It is very clear to the Armenians of Karabagh that their backs are to the
wall. As they see it, if they are attacked, their only choice is whether to die
on their feet or on their knees.

It is not clear whether Baku's cause, admittedly not a *jihad*, could draw international Islamist support of any weight. Most of the Chechens and Wahhabi militants spotted in Baku since the 1994 cease-fire, appear to be just passing through, in transit to or from the battlegrounds of the Balkans, Afghanistan, Chechnya or Iraq.

The situation is complicated by the fact that much of what Armenia imports from the outside world has to be hauled in from Iran on Iranian trucks owned and driven by ethnic Azeri citizens of Iran. They are always welcome in the markets of Yerevan.

The international organizations talk of peace, and meaningless resolution follows meaningless resolution, but no Azeri government is likely to renounce its claim to Nagorno-Karabagh and survive, and no Karabagh Armenian would ever dream of putting his head into the Baku lion's mouth.

At one time it seemed that the post-Soviet Conference for Security and Cooperation in Europe[110] might provide a forum for resolution of the Nagorno-Karabagh issue, until at the end of the CSCE meeting in Prague in January 1992, embarrassed delegates realized that they had just admitted two new members who were *de facto* at war with each other—Armenia and Azerbaijan.

A subsequent meeting in Helsinki led to proposals for a Minsk Conference to work out a peace agreement. The conference never took place, but more modest hopes centered on a Minsk Group, that actually met in Rome. Its efforts petered out in the summer of 1993.

Dr. Vafa Guluzade[111], an Azeri ideologue who witnessed the process, spoke of "completely incompetent ambassadors from France and other countries.... .taking part there without any knowledge of the region or the core of the conflict; without any tools to put pressure on the parties".

He may have been too hard on French diplomats who were under orders from the Quai d'Orsay not to make any commitment that would upset France's Armenian community, which is 300,000 strong and politically powerful enough to push through legislation which makes it a criminal offence in France to deny the Armenian genocide.

But Guluzade was genuinely aggrieved. Caspian oil gives his people a huge sense of entitlement, so there seems something very unjust in the way that voting blocks of *Diaspora* Armenians in the West, in France and California in particular, stand in the way of Azerbaijan's manifest destiny.[112]

Guluzade was an advisor to the late President Heidar Aliev and, like his old boss, a one-time agent of the Soviet KGB. He is reputed to be the author of the interesting 1998 *Decree of the President of Azerbaijan on the Genocide of the Azerbaijanis*[113]. This document, which has been compared to the *Protocols of the Learned Elders of Zion*[114] as a classic of racist fiction, argues that far from being responsible for the murder of a million or two Armenians, the Turkic peoples are, in fact, the victims. The *Decree* alleges that over the years the Armenians have murdered countless Azeris in a holocaust of Hitleresque scale.

◆        ◆        ◆

Even countries which make much of their claims to be good international citizens, turned their backs on Nagorno-Karabagh and its fight for survival. Territorial integrity is a sacred cow, even when preserving it leaves a people in the shadow of genocide.

If the *Karabaghtsi* are allowed to escape their fate, the Quebeckers, the Basques, the Corsicans, the Sikhs, all these people will see it as a precedent and may want out of their present arrangements. Much better to turn a blind eye and hope that the Azeris can achieve a final solution quickly and quietly, without embarrassing the international community.

Ruanda and Srebrenica have convinced the Armenians that the United Nations would not deter the Azeris from any new onslaught, although retrospective resolutions would most certainly be passed deploring the extermination of the people of Nagorno-Karabagh.

Fortunately for the people of Nagorno-Karabagh, the Armenian *Diaspora* plays a significant role in American politics, particularly in the state of California with its fifty-five electoral votes. That is a reality for both Democrat and Republican, a reality as compelling as Azeri oil.

On a less prosaic level, students of international affairs observe that in a world of failed states and institutions, the Nagorno-Karabagh Republic stands out as a success story, despite, or perhaps because of, the odds stacked against it.

But the importance of Azeri oil cannot be under-rated. For more than a century, the Caspian basin, centered on Baku, has been famous for its oilfields. Rich reserves of natural gas are also proven.

At the close of the 20$^{th}$ century, an important consideration for oil-dependent Western nations, had to be getting this oil and natural gas to market.

The northern pipeline through Dagestan and the Chechen war zone had already been attacked by terrorists, so the central routes from Baku to Tblisi to Ceyhan (BTC) on the Mediterranean for oil, and from Baku to Tblisi to Batumi (BTB) on the Black Sea for natural gas, attracted most Western interest.

Because of fears that the $3.6 billion BTC oil pipeline would provide saboteurs with an irresistible target, the pipeline has been buried for its entire 1,100-mile length, and is monitored with advanced surveillance equipment, including unmanned helicopters, as well as by well-armed vehicle and foot patrols.

Both the BTC oil pipeline and the BTB gas pipeline avoid Nagorno-Kara-bagh and Armenia by about 30 miles, for the Azeris will not ship fuel through Armenian territory.

Oil is, however, just one of several geopolitical factors at work in the Southern Caucasus. Alignments are shifting as Russia seeks to define its role in the 21st century, and as Iran sees itself caught in the pincers, between American-dominated Iraq and American-dominated Afghanistan, at a time when Shiite clerics watch uneasily as Sunni Wahhabis take the lead in Islam's confrontation with the Western infidel.

The Israelis, pondering the need to do in Iran what they did to Saddam Hussein's French-built Osirak nuclear reactor in 1981, stir up centrifugal disaffection among Iran's millions of Azeris, neighbors of ex-Soviet Azer-baijan, and of the Armenian republics, where two axes intersect.

Russia sees Armenia as its only friend in the Southern Caucasus, and as a bridge to Iran. The United States, Israel and Turkey, together with Geor-gia and Azerbaijan, keep cautious eyes on both Russia and Iran.

Natural as an alliance between Turk and Azeri might seem, even allowing for the Sunni-Shia divide, the fact that the victims of two great holocausts of the 20th century, Jews and Armenians, find themselves on opposite sides, seems incongruous.

Despite the West's thirst for oil and natural gas, and heavy investment in pipeline construction, the great powers have been unable to come to grips with issues that emerged in the Southern Caucasus after the Soviet Union collapsed.

# ENDNOTES

1. The figure is debated by Armenians and Turks as it is key to determining how many Armenians perished in the great slaughter that took place at the end of the 19<sup>th</sup> and beginning of the 20<sup>th</sup> centuries. Most Western scholars agree with the historian Arnold Toynbee that the number of Armenians in the Ottoman Empire at the start of the First World War was about two million.

2. Ankara long refused to recognize the politically uncomfortable existence of a distinct Kurdish people. The Turks called their Kurds "Mountain Turks" and have been at war with Kurdish militants since 1984. *Britannica.com* estimates that the Turkish army has killed about 30,000 Kurds in the last twenty years.

3. Blank, Stephen. *The Sorcerer as Apprentice: Stalin as Commissar of Nationalities, 1917–1924.* Contributions in Military Studies, vol.145. Westport, CT: Greenwood Press, 1994.

4. Sevastopol had been besieged by British and French in 1854–55, and by the Germans in 1941–42. What was lost in war was regained in peace. Then in 1954, Khrushchev, seeking to consolidate his grip on power, gave the Crimea to the Ukrainian Soviet Socialist Republic. Although three-quarters of Sevastopol's inhabitants are ethnic Russians, the Russian Federation now has to negotiate with an independent Ukraine for use of the base.

5. Energy Information Administration, August 2003. Natural gas reserves are estimated to be between 232 and 327 trillion cubic feet, ref. http://www.eia.doe.gov.

6. Although U.S.-Iranian relations had been fraught since the fall of the Shah, so great was Tehran's antipathy to the Taliban regime that during Operation Enduring Freedom in the immediate post 9–11 period, Iran offered the Americans use of certain Iranian airfields for the recovery of battle-damaged aircraft.

7. After the December 1994 raid on Grozny which the Chechens refer to as "Yeltsin's Bay of Pigs", Chechen leader Dzhokhar M. Dudaev (1944–96) concluded that it was time he sought assistance outside the former Soviet Union, and turned to Saudi-based fundamentalists. Today, the term Wahhabi is used by people with little understanding of Islam, particularly in Russia, to describe any Sunni extremist.

8. The Soviet Union, which would formally unite Armenia and Azerbaijan with Russia for the first time since the fall of the Tsar, was not established until December 1922, so the Caucasian Bureau of the Russian Communist Party had no legal basis in July 1921 on which to override the November 1920 decision of the Azerbaijan Revolutionary Committee, assigning three regions to Armenia: Nagorno-Karabagh, the southern Armenian province of Zangezur, and Nakhichevan. In July 1923, prompted by Stalin, the Azerbaijan Revolutionary Committee annexed Nagorno-Karabagh and seized Nakhichevan a year later.

9. Hiro, Dilip. *Between Marx and Muhammad: The Changing Face of Central Asia*. London: HarperCollins, 1995.

10. Hopkirk, Peter. *On Secret Service East of Constantinople*. London: John Murray, 1994.

11. Orhan Pamuk (1952-), best-selling Turkish novelist and winner of the 2006 Nobel Prize in Literature, often vilified at home for his call for an objective examination of the genocide issue.

12. Taner Akçam's book, *A Shameful Act—the Armenian Genocide and the Question of Turkish Responsibility* (New York, Henry Holt and Co., 2006) is the first objective study of the genocide issue based on Turkish sources. Professor Akçam (1953-) teaches at the Center for Holocaust and Genocide Studies at the University of Minnesota.

13. Heidar Aliev (1923–2003) was described by Zhores A. Medvedev (*Andropov: An Insider's Account of Power and Politics Within the Kremlin.* London: Penguin, 1983) as a tough man, a good administrator, and personally honest. In 1967 he became head of the KGB in Azerbaijan. Two years later Brezhnev made him First Secretary of the Azerbaijan Central Committee. He was so successful in eradicating a culture of corruption and misrule in the republic, that people joked that Aliev had "restored Soviet power" in Azerbaijan. In 1982, Andropov, who also made his name in the KGB, appointed him to the Politburo as a First Deputy Prime Minister. It did no harm that he was a nominal Moslem at a time when the Soviet Union was becoming increasingly aware of the Moslem world within and beyond its borders, but Aliev was no mere token.

14. Former CIA Director George Tenet claimed that Clinton slashed the budget for the CIA's clandestine service by 25 per cent at a time when the agency was trying to penetrate Osama bin Laden's organization, in addition to monitoring other threats to United States' interests (*At the Center of the Storm: My Years at the CIA.* New York: HarperCollins, 2007).

15. Many of these came in the guise of missionaries preaching Iran's particular brand of Shiism, but in the case of a theocracy like Tehran's, the line between evangelist and political agent may not be clear.

16. This total is about ten times that for the San Francisco earthquake and fire of 1906.

17. William Allan. Private communication.

18. Kocharian, born in1954, grew up in Stepanakert, then served in the Soviet Army. He graduated with honors from the Yerevan Polytechnic, and became a Party *apparatchnik* in Stepanakert's silk factory. He was elected to Armenia's supreme soviet before the Karabagh War, then fought in the Shoushi campaign. He came to power in Stepanakert during the dark days of August 1992 and was elected president of the Nagorno-Karabagh Republic in December 1994. A quietly persistent man, he neither smokes nor drinks.

19. The U.N. High Commissioner for Refugees reported that at the end of 2005 there were still about 219,550 people considered refugees or displaced persons in Armenia, where the government has granted them citizenship and attempted to provide all with permanent housing. (*2005 Global Refugee Trends*, June 2006.)

20. Dr. Leila Yunusova, writing for the Institute for War and Peace Reporting in 1996, says that about 185,000 Azeris left Armenia at the start of the war, and that a further 520,000 fled from Nagorno-Karabagh or from the NKR buffer zone.

21. The United Nations put the December 2005 total at 581,500. *Op cit.*

22. "Red Bridge to Nowhere." *Sobaka*, 23 January 2003.

23. De Waal, Thomas. *Black Garden—Armenia and Azerbaijan through Peace and War*. New York: New York University Press, 2004. The International Crisis Group and *CIA World Factbook* estimates are in the 13 to 16 per cent range. (CRS Report for Congress on Armenia, Azerbaijan and Georgia: Security Issues and Implications for U.S. Interests—updated February 2007).

24. Karapetian, Samvel. *Armenian Cultural Monuments in the Region of Karabagh, Book III*. Yerevan: Gitutiun Publishing House, 2001.

25. De Waal. *Op cit.*

26. Most other Kurds are Moslem, but the Yezidis fear and worship Meleke Tawus, a dark, female angel who must be appeased, rather than Allah. The Yezidis believe that God, the Creator, gave them over to Meleke Tawus. The term Yezidi is derived from a Sumerian phrase meaning "one who follows the true path".

27. By late 1917 the Germans had occupied Tblisi and their Turkish allies were advancing on Baku. Although there was some tension between Germans and Turks, the British feared the two columns would concentrate and drive through Persia to threaten India, perhaps triggering a new Indian Mutiny. Dunsterforce, whose eventual nucleus was the British 39th Brigade, was commanded by Maj.Gen. L.C. Dunsterville, a Russian-speaking officer of the Indian Army. It was formed to block any such move and to protect British interests in the Caspian oilfields. In June 1918, the force captured Bandar-e Anzali on the Caspian and embarked for Baku. It withdrew 14 September as Mursal Pasha took the city, returning to Baku as an occupation force after the November Armistice.

28. The Soviet regime named Stepanakert, capital of Nagorno-Karabagh, in honor of Stepan Shaumian (1878–1918).

29. From the Arabic *fida'i,* meaning one who is ready to sacrifice his life for a cause.

30. Sometimes called *djogads*, or hunting parties—another term dating from the genocide years.

31. Most *kontraktniki* were freelance, or informal groups of freelancers, rather than employees of private military corporations, as has become the norm in Afghanistan and Iraq.

32. A Category A Motor Rifle Division of 13,294 personnel had three mechanized rifle regiments (2 BTR and 1 BMP), an artillery regiment, a tank battalion (94 T-72s) and often an independent tank battalion (with another 51 main battle tanks), as well as the usual missile, anti-tank, recon, helicopter, engineer, etc., units. The 31$^{st}$ Guards Motor Rifle Division was Category B, which meant that it was at between 50 and 75 per cent strength.

33. For obvious reasons, many of those who transferred their allegiance prefer that their full names not appear in print.

34. The Blue Berets or Airborne Forces, the Vozdushno-Desantniye Voiska (VDV), are the unquestioned elite of the Russian Army, inheriting a tradition that goes back to the "deep operations" concepts of Marshal Mikhail Nikolayevich Tukhachevsky (1893–1937).

35. *Boston Globe*, 16 March 1992.

36. Including Marshals Ivan Baghramian, Hamazasp Babayanian, Sergei Khudyakov (Khamferyants), and Admiral Ivan Isakov.

37. Before the Russian Revolution, the Russians used the term Tartar to refer to various populations of Asiatic origin, ranging from the Azeris, to Tartars of the Volga, and to Siberians. It was, however, the term generally applied to the Shiite Moslems of Azerbaijan. Most of the other "Tartars" are Sunni.

38. *Dyedovshchina* is the name given to the informal system of bullying of new recruits in the Russian armed services, MVD, and border guards, by men in the last year of service. The term is derived from *dyed* (grandfather), with the suffix—*shchina* which indicates attribution, as in *Yezhovshchina*. In 1967, cohorts of three-year and two-year conscripts were present in the Soviet army at the same time, and *dyedovshchina* emerged, or was greatly exacerbated by tensions that developed then.

39. Shamil Salmanovich Basayev (1965–2006) was born in Chechnya. By 1991 he had become active in Caucasian Islamic movements. After fighting in Abkhazia, Basayev moved on to Azerbaijan, where according to some sources, he led a battalion-strength Chechen contingent. According to Azeri Colonel Azer Rustamov, in 1992, "Hundreds of Chechen volunteers rendered us invaluable help in these battles, led by Shamil Basayev and Salman Raduev." Basayev was one of the last fighters to leave Shoushi. He later said that he and his battalion had only lost only one battle and that that defeat was inflicted by the *Dashnak* battalion. He left Karabagh claiming that the Azeris were not engaged in a legitimate *jihad*. He subsequently fought in the 1992–93 Abkhazian War. During the First Chechen War (1994–96) he led the raid that resulted in the hostage-taking at Budennovsk. Invading Dagestan in 1999, he launched the Second Chechen War, losing a foot when he stepped on a mine. He subsequently claimed responsibility for the Dubrovka Theatre incident in 2002, and for the 2004 school raid in Beslan, North Ossetia. Basayev had a price of more than $10-million on his head when he was killed in an explosion in Ingushetia.

40. Lavrenti Pavlovich Beria (1899–1953) headed the NKVD from 1938 until Stalin's death, when other Soviet leaders feared that he was poised to seize power and moved against him.

41. Libaridian, Gerard J. (ed.). *The Karabagh File: Documents and Facts on the Region of Mountainous Karabagh, 1918–1988.* Cambridge, Zoryan Institute for Contemporary Armenian Research and Documentation, 1988).

42. Armenians also believe that the feast of *Qurban Bairam* was the occasion for the massacre of Shoushi's Armenian population in March 1920.

43. Abulfaz Aliev Elchibey (1938–2000), leader of the Azerbaijan Popular Front, elected president of Azerbaijan on 7 June 1992. He fled Baku a year

later under pressure from Surat Husseinov and Heidar Aliev (no relation, although both Alievs came from Nakhichevan).

44. Epstein, Julius. *Operation Keelhaul: The Story of Forced Repatriation.* Old Greenwich, CT: Devin-Adair, 1974; and Sanders, James D., Mark A. Sauter, and R. Cort Kirkwood. *Soldiers of Misfortune: Washington's Secret Betrayal of American POWs in the Soviet Union.* Washington: National Press Books, 1992.

45. Gen. Pavel Sergeyevich Grachev (1948-) was Yeltsin's defense minister from May 1992 to June 1996, and instigator of Russia's first Chechnya adventure.

46. Ayaz Niyaziyevich Mutalibov (1938-), Communist Party official elected first president of independent Azerbaijan in May 1990, but ousted 6 March 1992 after the loss of Khodjali. Briefly regained power in May. Widely seen as Moscow's man.

47. After three generations of secular Soviet rule, many Azeris no longer honored the Islamic taboo against alcohol.

48. Although largely superseded by firearms in the closing years of the Middle Ages, the crossbow had been used for silent killing during the Second World War by agents of the Special Operations Executive, and by Australian forces and *Montagnard* militiamen in the jungles of the Far East.

49. Armenia is now the focus of the CIS regional air defense system.

50. De Waal, Thomas, *op cit.*

51. The firebase or fire-support base (FSB) evolved in the Vietnam War in the context of warfare fought without defined front lines by infantry often far from other support. Infantry were able to radio for a fire mission from

the nearest available battery, which might be located in a heavily fortified and well-defended firebase, or from some much more rough-and-ready position. With the exceptions of Khodjali, Shoushi and Aghdam, the Azeri firebases had an ad hoc look about them and tended to plan their own fire missions rather than respond to operational requirements.

52. The highest organizational level of the Armenian army is actually the brigade, which has between 1,500 and 2,500 troops, organized in three or four battalions.

53. In 1995 the Russians signed a 25-year lease on their Gyumri base, and two years later, a comprehensive Treaty on Friendship, Cooperation and Mutual Assistance with Armenia. The Russian 7th Army is still well-positioned to guard Russia's southern flank against any Turkish or Iranian threat.

54. While the 31st was Category B, the 6th, 75th and 216th Divisions were Category C, which meant that they were at between 5 and 50 per cent of nominal strength, with older equipment. They would need two months to mobilize. Category B divisions, with their modern equipment, should be battle-ready within a few days. The 104th Guards Airborne Division, was of course, like all Soviet airborne units, Category A, or combat ready.

55. The withdrawal of four divisions of the Soviet 4th Army from Azerbaijan was officially completed in May 1993, a year before the cease-fire.

56. Azerbaijan did not finally accede to the Confederation of Independent States until Heidar Aliev came to power in the Autumn of 1993. In 1999, Azerbaijan, with Georgia and Uzbekistan, pulled out of the CIS collective security pact.

57. Bekesi, Laszlo. *Soviet Uniforms & Militaria 1917–1991*. Marlborough, Wilts: Crowood Press, 2000.

58. During the Soviet era, the Baku regime had been wholly successful in "cleansing" Nakhichevan of it's once significant Armenian population; there are no Armenians there now. This provided the blueprint for what was intended in Nagorno-Karabagh. Both Elchibey and the family of Heidar Aliev came from Nakhichevan and were familiar with what had been done there. Today, Nakhichevan's main importance, bordering both Iran and Turkey, is as a trans-shipment point for Afghan heroin.

59. Elena Georgiyevna Bonner (1923-), twice wounded as a battlefield nurse during the Great Patriotic War, and subsequently a pediatrician, and a human rights activist and author.

60. Alikhanov was a friend of Anastas Mikoyan and knew Lavrenti Beria and Semyon Ter-Petrosian. He had played a major role in establishing Soviet power in the Southern Caucasus. Sakharov, Andrei. *Memoirs.* New York, Alfred A. Knopf, 1990; and Andrew, Christopher, and Oleg Gordievsky. *KGB—The Inside Story.* London, Hodder & Stoughton, 1990.

61. The threat of terrorism was one of a number of factors in the mid-1980s, that led the Soviet MVD to establish a unit and train its men in some of the rough-and-tumble skills of the West German GSG-9, British SAS, and American Green Berets. These were the *Otdiela Militsii Osobovo Nazacheniya* (OMON)—Special Purpose Police Troops. As a sign of respect for the citizens of the "first socialist state", the Soviet Militia had always worn formal uniforms on duty; the OMON, however, wore blue-black combat clothing. The Azeri interior ministry's own OMON corps was later renamed OPON (the P standing for *Politsii)*, and was implicated in abortive coups against the Aliev regime in October 1994 and March 1995. These coups may have been instigated by the pro-Turkish Gray Wolves.

62. *Conflict in the Soviet Union: Black January in Azerbaijan.* New York: Helsinki Watch/Memorial Report, May 1991.

63. Odom, Lt.Gen. William E. *The Collapse of the Soviet Military.* New Haven, CT: Yale University Press, 1998.

64. Dr. Levon A. Ter-Petrosian (1945-) was a leader of the Karabagh Committee and from December 1988 to May 1989, was under arrest together with other members. In August 1989, he was elected to the supreme soviet of the Armenian SSR, and a year later became chairman. Ter-Petrosian was elected the first president of the newly-independent Republic of Armenia on 16 October 1991 and re-elected 22 September 1996. His popularity waned when he sold Armenian electrical capacity to Georgia while rationing electricity in Armenia to four hours per day. This was in order to fund a war against Azerbaijan—a move considered necessary by the Armenian army. He lost more support when he banned the leading opposition party, the Armenian Revolutionary Federation, the *Dashnakstutiun,* jailed its leadership, and shut down its newspaper *Yerkir,* the country's largest daily. He was forced to step down in February 1998 after advocating concessions to Azerbaijan.

65. *Propiski* were the internal passports intended to keep Soviet citizens where Moscow thought they should be. In this instance, there were fears that *fedayner* from Armenia were moving into Nagorno-Karabagh to cause trouble for the Baku authorities.

66. Shoushi had withstood two sieges by Persian armies, in 1795 and 1826.

67. The terms Tartar (or Tatar) and Azeri both refer to the same Turkic-speaking Shiite community, whose homeland lies west of the Caspian. Since the creation of the Azerbaijan SSR, the latter term is generally preferred south of the Great Caucasus.

68. A Tartar or Azeri soldier; from the Arabic *askar* (plural *askari*), meaning spearman or soldier.

69. The *Strela* (SA-7 Grail) is a man-portable, low-altitude, surface-to-air missile system, comparable to the U.S. Redeye. It has a passive infrared homing device and a contact fuze. It went into service in 1968 and was used to some effect in Vietnam and in the Yom Kippur War. Currently in service with Chechen insurgents, Taliban, Al Quaeda, Hezbollah, etc.

70. Baroness Caroline Cox of Queensbury, Deputy Speaker of the British House of Lords, described what she observed in *Christianity Today*, April 1998, Vol.42, No.5.

71. PsyWar, psychological warfare, involves a range of approaches to undermine enemy morale or simply scare the enemy to the point at which his effectiveness is significantly reduced.

72. The BMP-1 is a well-armored, amphibious infantry combat vehicle, mounting a 73 mm 2A20 short-recoil gun which fires the same munition as the RPG-7, an AT-3c (Sagger) anti-tank missile launching rail, and coaxial 7.62 mm machine gun. The BMP-2 was designed to supplement the BMP-1 rather than replace it, and has a similar chassis. It relies on a low silhouette for protection, having rather thin armor. The rear doors are hollow and serve as diesel tanks. The BMP-2 mounts a 30 mm 2A42 auto-cannon, an AT-5 (Spandrel) wire-guided anti-tank missile launcher, and 7.62 mm coaxial machine gun. Both vehicles have crews of three and can carry a section of infantry. Both saw service in Afghanistan in the 1980s.

73. Gaziev was prominent in the Azerbaijan Popular Front, but had strong Russian connections which his pro-Turkish colleagues might have considered useful. He was a friend of Grachev's.

74. Small enough to be carried through Soviet railroad tunnels, relatively fast, and easily serviced by conscript crews, the 41-ton T-72 is, however, poorly armored and under-gunned. In the 1982 Lebanon campaign that Israel called *Operation Peace for Galilee,* Syrian T-72 units were badly mauled by Yanush Ben Gal's 63-ton Merkavas and by the Israeli Air

Force's Cobra gunships. In the Iraq wars Saddam Hussein's T-72s were completely outclassed by the American 61½-ton Abrams.

75. Later in the Karabagh war, Azeri armor was often decorated with the star and crescent of the Azerbaijan flag, but there is no record of this marking having been used at Shoushi.

76. Entered production in 1966 and still in service in the 21$^{st}$ century. The T-72 and all subsequent Russian tanks were developed from the T-64.

77. The 125 mm D-81 gun comes close to overloading the T-72's small chassis. It can theoretically push its finned rounds out at 1800 m/sec at full charge, although a muzzle-velocity of 1700 m/sec might be more usual in a combat environment. The D-81 is used on T-64, T-72, T-80 and T-90 Soviet/Russian tanks.

78. The flag of the Nagorno-Karabagh Republic differs from Armenia's blue, red and orange horizontal tricolor only in that a stepped section of the fly, outlined in white and pointing toward the hoist, represents Artsakh and the aspiration of its people to join with their kinfolk in the Republic of Armenia.

79. One of these smart bombs, targeted by a reconnaissance Su24MR (Fencer) and a Su-25 (Frogfoot) working in tandem, on a signal from his own satellite phone, killed Chechen President Dzhokhar Dudayev 21 April 1996. As a former air force general, he should have known better than to use a satellite phone when the Sukhois were overhead.

80. CIS leaders met at Tashkent and agreed on distribution of Soviet arms to successor states. Azerbaijan, although not at this time a CIS member, was to receive weapons and equipment from the 31$^{st}$ (Gandža) and 6$^{th}$ (Lenkoran) Motor Rifle Divisions of the 4$^{th}$ Army, including 150 tanks, 290 armored fighting vehicles, 150 mortars, and 90 anti-aircraft guns. The

Azeris proceeded to take over air bases and aircraft, and part of the Caspian Sea Flotilla.

81. The NATO combined arms operation involves seven Battlefield Operating Systems—maneuver, air defense, artillery support, mobility and counter-mobility, command, military intelligence, and logistics. Russian army doctrine puts particularly heavy emphasis on the use of artillery—seizing the initiative and retaining fire superiority, and on the coordinated maneuvering of mechanized infantry and tank units to outflank and envelop enemy formations.

82. The two types of *Igla* (the SA-16 Gimlet and the SA-18 Grouse) are Man-Portable Air Defense Systems (MANPADS) and have smaller but more lethal warheads than the *Strela*, also used during the campaign. *Igla* warheads have both impact and proximity fuses and their infra-red-seekers are designed to distinguish between targets and countermeasures, such as flares. Low-trajectory range is about 3 miles and the *Igla* can engage targets as high as 11,000 feet. The *Igla* is comparable to the American Stinger.

83. Hasratian, Lt.Col. Senor. *General Ivanian.* Yerevan: Amaras, 2004.

84. Ivanian had two of the famous Karabagh horses who were adept at finding their way safely through the minefields that made travel dangerous in the forward areas.

85. Shahen Meghrian (1952–93), a *Dashnak* from Gyulistan, had been an economist before the war.

86. The Lebanese Civil War lasted intermittently from 1975 to 1990.

87. Although St. Gregory the Illuminator is considered to be the Apostle to the Armenians, having baptized King Trdat IV at some time between 301 and 314, St. Juda (or Jude Thaddeus) and St. Bartholomew brought Christianity to Armenia, then a client kingdom of Persia, in the first cen-

tury. The Armenian Apostolic Church is so called in reference to these men. According to the Armenian tradition, around 65, St. Juda was martyred together with the apostle Simon the Canaanite, with whom he is usually associated.

88. This force was formed in Karabagh. It drove south through the Lachin Corridor into Armenia, west along the Saravan road, north through the Selim Pass to Lake Sevan, and finally east over the Zod Pass into Karvachar—a distance of 150 miles, over very mountainous country and over some roads that don't appear on any map. Such is the geography of the Southern Caucasus.

89. Azeri sources claim that radio intercepts confirm that mountain troops of the 7th Russian Army's 128th Regiment, based in Armenia, were also involved in the attack, although Russian communications security, properly implemented, should prevent identification of units. See Mekhtiev, Aidin. "Armiyanskiye Voiska Zanyali Kel'badzhar." *Nezavisimaya Gazeta*, Moscow, 6 April, 1994, page 3.

90. Goltz, Thomas. *Azerbaijan: A Journey of Discovery and Despair in a Post-Soviet State.* New York: M.E.Sharpe, 1997.

91. The 104th had a "first in, last out " tradition. In December 1979, units of the division had seized the Kabul/Bagram Airfield, the city of Kandahar, and the strategically important Salang Pass, spearheading the Soviet occupation of Afghanistan.

92. The withdrawal of the Russian forces from Azerbaijan created a number of problems. It was not only the army that left. In September 1992, most of the two KGB Frontier Guard battalions and the MVD's 3,600-strong Don Division, which had protected Azerbaijan's frontier with Iran, were withdrawn, and had to be replaced by Azeri troops. The Azeris also found that mere possession of the ex-Soviet Sukhoi and Ilyushin aircraft they inherited after the Tashkent agreement, did not amount to an air

defense system capable of keeping Iranian F-14A Tomcats out of Azeri skies. This put further pressure on the Baku government, as did the centrifugal tendencies of Nakhichevan Azeris, and the Lezgin and Talish minorities. The immediate air defense problem was, however, largely solved by the Turkish 2$^{nd}$ Tactical Air Force. Turkish F-16C/D Vipers (aka Fighting Falcons) are more dangerous than the Iranian F-14As, whose rate and radius of turn, thrust-to-weight ratio, and aerodynamic characteristics, would leave them at a comparative disadvantage (the last two U.S. Navy F-14D Tomcat squadrons were deactivated in 2006). Capable of 9-g turns, the F-16 Viper would be a formidable opponent in a dogfight over the disputed southern Caspian. In January 2002, Azerbaijan reluctantly signed a 10-year lease that allows the Russians to station up to 1,500 personnel at the Gabala radar site.

93. Some of Heidar Aliev's enemies, and he had many, encouraged rumors that he had, in fact, been born in Armenia. No one inferred from this, however, that he entertained any sympathies for the Armenian cause.

94. The subsequent emergence of Vladimir V. Putin can be seen as evidence to the extent to which former officers of the Soviet KGB continue to influence developments in Russia.

95. Moscow agreed to Gaziev's extradition to Baku in April 1996 in order to placate Heidar Aliev.

96. Azerbaijan's post-Soviet parliament. Pursuant to his agreement with Surat Husseinov, Heidar Aliev was chairman of the body.

97. Russian troops invaded Chechnya in December 1994.

98. In February 2003, the United States listed Gulbuddin Hekmatyar (1947-) as a "specially designated global terrorist" under Executive Order 13224.

99. Auerbach, Jon. "Azerbaijan Hires Afghan Mujahideen to Fight Armenia." *Boston Globe*, 8 November 1993.

100. Mark Irkali, et al. in "God Save the Shah" (*Sobaka*, 22 May 2003), present evidence that some, at least, of Aliev's *mujahidin* were far from being the veteran guerrillas who had driven the Russians out of Afghanistan.

101. Paktia has a reputation as a breeding-ground for mercenaries, but its people are Pashto-speaking Hanafi Sunnis, and there are no reports of such in Azerbaijan during the Karabagh War.

102. Details of the American involvement are obscure, but the names of two former USAF generals, Richard V. Secord (1932-) and Harry C. Aderholt (1920-), and a MEGA Oil Co. executive Gary Best, have been mentioned as friends of Azerbaijan. Aderholt is said to have advised Baku to make a formal request for an American "mobile training team" of advisors—a request that was rejected. Subsequently, Secord and Aderholt withdrew from the operation, and Best and a team of active or retired U.S. Special Forces operatives are reported to have stage-managed the recruitment and deployment of the Afghan mercenaries. See: Goltz, Thomas. *Azerbaijan Diary: A Rogue Reporter's Adventures in an Oil-Rich, War-Torn, Post-Soviet Republic*. Armonk, NY: Sharpe, 1999.

103. Daniel Schneider. "Afghan Fighters Join Azeri-Armenian War." *Christian Science Monitor,* 16 November 1993, p.7.

104. Pashto and Dari are the two principal languages of Afghanistan. Dari is the somewhat archaic Afghan variant of the Farsi spoken in Iran. The Hazaras speak a Dari dialect.

105. Dr. Leila Yunusova, who had been Azerbaijan's deputy defense minister in the 1992–93 Popular Front administration, blamed Sadyquov for

the defeat, according to Abbasov, Idrak and Jasur Mamedov. "Azeri Veterans Recall Military Fiasco." CRS No. 219, 21 January, 2004.

106. According to an unnamed Western diplomat in Baku, quoted in *The Washington Post* on 11 August 1993: "They would be almost unopposed. This city is defenseless."

107. To the north lies Russia and to the south Iran, so that any flights from the United States or Europe are restricted to this narrow corridor.

108. Energy secretary from 18 August 1998 to 20 January 2001.

109. Croissant, Michael P. *The Armenia-Azerbaijan Conflict*. Westport, CT: Praeger, 1998.

110. The CSCE became the Organization for Security and Cooperation in Europe (OSCE) after its December 1994 meeting in Budapest.

111. Vafa Guluzade (1940-) graduated from Azerbaijan University in 1963 and received his doctorate from the Oriental Studies Institute of the Academy of Sciences in Moscow in 1967. He began his career in the Soviet Ministry of Foreign Affairs and later served in embassies in Egypt and Algeria. In addition to Azeri and Russian, he speaks English and Arabic, and has interpreted for Brezhnev, Kosygin, and Gromyko among others. He has been deeply involved with the negotiations on Nagorno-Karabakh, leading delegations to meetings in Rome, Paris, Vienna, Prague, Geneva, Brussels, Ankara and Moscow. He has also argued strongly that Azerbaijan offer to provide facilities for United States bases.

112. Azerbaijan could generate over $2-billion a year through oil production royalties. See: Cohen, Dr. Ariel. "The New Great Game: Oil Politics in the Caucasus and Central Asia." Heritage Foundation Backgrounder No. 1065, 25 January 1996.

113. The text of the *Decree* is available online from the official website of the Office of the President of Azerbaijan at http://www.zerbaijan.com/azeri/genocide.htm.

114. The *Protocols* appear to have been authored in 1903 by the KGB's precursor, the Tsarist *Okhrana*, with the intention of directing popular discontent away from the regime and against Russia's Jewish community. They were largely plagiarized from Maurice Joly's 1864 "Dialogues in Hell", an anti-Bonapartist diatribe.

978-0-595-48679-3
0-595-48679-7

Lightning Source UK Ltd.
Milton Keynes UK
UKOW04f2121151215

264761UK00001B/282/P